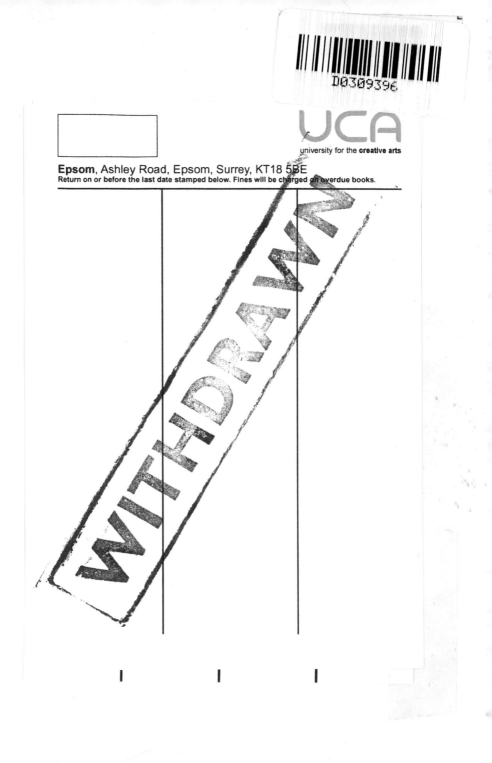

"Stan Sauerhaft and Chris Atkins, two veterans of the corporate positioning wars, have written a thoughtful, no-holds-barred, eminently readable explanation of how to manage corporate image and maintain corporate impact. Their sound and straightforward advice can be applied to any organization, in numerous situations—from corporate culture to consumerism, from self promotions to self preservation. If you want to know how to really manage perceptions—shape them, mold them, steer them toward your own goals—read this book."

FRASER P. SEITEL
Senior Vice President
Director, Public Affairs
The Chase Manhattan Bank, N.A.

"*Image Wars* tells executives how best to present their company to those who watch it. Stan Sauerhaft and Chris Atkins have written a book every executive should read."

CHARLES F. LUCE
Director, Metropolitan Life Insurance Co.
former Chairman of Con Edison

"An engagingly written guide book . . . Sauerhaft and Atkins demonstrate persuasively the effectiveness of communicating a ready concern and cooperation for the company's customers, clients and community as an on-going mode of doing business in an increasingly fractious and litigious marketplace. . . . They offer [many tools] by which to build credibility and respect for the company."

AUSTIN S. MURPHY
Chairman
East River Savings Bank

"If the work of Sauerhaft and Atkins were part of the manuals of corporations forty and fifty years ago, companies would have avoided many of the troubles which beset them. . . . Required reading for all executives for better understanding of their rights and obligations to their various constituents . . ."

FRED SULLIVAN
Chairman
Interim Systems

"*Image Wars* is an excellent guide for any thoughtful executive seeking to deal with the communications challenges facing his business."

JOHN LARSEN
Past President of The Bowery Savings Bank and former Chairman of the Citizen's Budget Commission

---

Image Wars

Protecting Your Company When There's No Place To Hide

STAN SAUERHAFT

CHRIS ATKINS

A Philip Lief Group Book

WILEY

John Wiley & Sons

New York Chichester Brisbane Toronto Singapore

ISBN 0-471-60936-6

Printed in the United States of America

10 9 8 7 6 5 4 3 2 1

Preface

Image Wars: Why Fight?

"Why should I worry about my corporate image?"

That's a question we're frequently asked, and it's not always easy to answer.

Most executives seem to understand intuitively that a good corporate image is worth having, but when asked to quantify its importance to the corporation's success, they come up dry. They're in good company.

To our knowledge, almost no research has ever been done to show just how a good or bad image affects sales, the barometer by which most external communications (public relations, advertising, sales promotion and so forth) are measured. Efforts to quantify the correlation are usually not fruitful.

Suppose, for the sake of argument, that *Fortune* magazine's annual list of most admired companies is an acceptable gauge of corporate image, at least among businessmen. If one tracks these entries' annual rise and fall over a period of five years, and then tracks those same companies against the Fortune 500 lists of companies by size for the same period, one will quickly realize that there appears to be no correlation between image and sales. In fact, in some cases, companies that show continuous improvement among the Fortune 500 have simultaneously dropped lower and lower on the "Most Admired" list. Most of the companies in the Fortune top 100 have never even been on the "Most Admired" list.

One might draw the conclusion, then, that corporate image is not too important. Why fight the Image Wars?

Taking the time and trouble to nurture and protect your corporate image is the same as putting money in the bank for the proverbial rainy day. Your corporate image *can* support product sales, but its real value is in affording the company a bank account of credibility with audiences beyond just customers.

As we'll see early on, one of the biggest challenges facing companies today is the protection of the environment. If your company's reputation is that of a polluter, you may have a hard time getting approval to expand your plant site or move into a new community.

Another case: If your company is seen as uncaring or aloof from the community, don't count on the support of towns-people or local legislators should a corporate raider launch a hostile takeover of your company.

No Place To Hide

Today, companies truly have no place to hide. Activists, gadflies, legislators and regulators—even your own employees—are watching more closely than ever to see if your company is an asset to the community or a decided liability. Each of these audiences, and many others, has a vested interest in how your company behaves. New legislation, such as SARA Title III (discussed in some detail in Chapter 10) makes it easier than ever for these potential adversaries to know exactly what you're doing behind the plant fence. If they don't like what they see, they can literally shut you down.

Is there hope? As we point out throughout the book, many companies have learned how to neutralize adversaries and even convert them into supporters through a carefully orchestrated communications plan that tangibly and visibly demonstrates concern for the well-being of all of these constituents.

Does all of this amount to a war? It certainly seems like a war when the Environmental Protection Agency accuses your company of pollution, or when a lunatic tampers with your products. And, just as nations have become preoccupied with *preparing* for war, much of the work you'll do to enhance your corporate image is preparatory. You may realize immediate benefits, but the greatest value of a strong positive image is the credibility it gives you when you need it most: when you need a few friends.

In the end, the value of your image *can* be measured in terms of sales: a good one can make the difference between having and not having any sales at all. What's that worth to you?

STAN SAUERHAFT
CHRIS ATKINS

New York, New York
December 1988

Acknowledgments

We are especially grateful to several people whose help was invaluable in the evolution of this book.

Jim Lindheim of Burson-Marsteller/London, who knows more about more things that just about anybody in our profession, was of particular help with sections on the environment and the Washington scene.

Various people within the Burson-Marsteller/New York office provided anecdotes, suggestions, and encouragement, but we want to particularly note here Maureen Aquaro, Bob Hope, Trudi Schutz, Mary-Ann Sherman, and Jonathan Williams.

Finally, our biggest thanks to Rosalie Sauerhaft and Janet Atkins—our toughest and most helpful editors.

S.S.
C.A.

Contents

Contents

1

Perception Versus Reality

Image and the Marketplace

Chapter 1

We hear a lot about corporate image these days, and much of what we hear is incorrect. Usually, corporate image is talked about as if it were a unilateral, inarguable concept meaning the same thing to everyone. If only it were that simple.

Corporate image is what people conjure up when they think of a company. No matter how hard you try to depict your company as one thing, people often see something else, depending on their perspective.

Think of your corporate image as a mosaic. From a distance, the mosaic forms a coherent picture. Close up, it appears to be no more than an agglomeration of tiles, with some tiles sparkling for attention and others dimmed. Unfortunately, most people draw conclusions about your company based on the close-up view, the small number of tiles they can see from their very limited perspective. For them, that fragment of the whole is your corporate image.

Does it matter if people base their opinion of your company on this small fragment? After all, that should make it easier to ensure that what they see is positive.

Generally, this is true, but not everyone looks at the same fragment, and even those who do may interpret what they see in different ways. Some people will see a few tiles and decide that the company is "red." Others will only remember "square." In more realistic terms, investors may see good earnings and think positively about the company; environmentalists may see thousands of gallons of sludge pouring from a company conduit and share a different sentiment altogether.

Corporate image is acutely important because it greatly influences public opinion about your company, and public opinion is the final judge of right/wrong, good/bad, and moral/immoral actions. In our society, public opinion is one of the most formidable phenomena a company encounters because so many powerful people are beholden to it—people who can protect you and people who can bring you down.

How frustrating, then, that public opinion toward your company can be shaped by such incomplete information! But that's the power of opinions.

Most of our decisions are based on opinions, and we are forced to form opinions on appallingly few facts. Rarely do we have incontrovertible evidence on which to base an objective decision; even a seemingly simple decision becomes overly complicated if one takes into account all of the facts.

For example, you go to the grocery store to buy cola. You can select from several leading brands. How should you choose?

You want to pick the best, so you begin by reviewing how the company's stock performs on the market. What about its policy on South Africa? Has the company contributed to public television? Does it advertise on violent, soft-porn network shows? Has management been fair with its unions? Remember, one of the company's delivery trucks nearly ran you off the road last month.

Ludicrous? On the surface, maybe, but a lot of purchase

decisions can be traced to answers to questions like those: The answers help crystallize an image of the company in the consumer's mind. Of course, most people would include in their decision how the product tastes: No matter how socially responsible a company may be, it will have a difficult time selling its cola if the stuff tastes like carbonated dishwater. But where there may be scant differences between products, other factors can have a great influence.

So each year, cola companies spend tens of millions of dollars allying themselves with causes, celebrities, and events to create the favorable impressions needed to influence purchase decisions. It often works—and not just for cola companies. Many New Yorkers have driven out of their way to buy Texaco gasoline because of the company's long-time support of the Metropolitan Opera, and many more public television viewers feel the same loyalty to Mobil. Yet few of us can say with authority that either brand of gasoline is better than the other—in fact, few of us really care.

It makes sense that if such a phenomenon can work in a company's favor, it can also be detrimental. Many people won't buy Texaco gas because they feel the company acted abominably during its protracted struggle with Pennzoil over Getty Oil. That purchase decision has nothing to do with the quality of Texaco products.

Smaller companies are just as subject to the vagaries of "image" as the Fortune 500. Suppose you run a small publicly traded Midwestern company called Spotso. Spotso makes a highly successful spot cleaner called Spot-So-Long, which is the market leader in the Midwest and is doing well elsewhere. While most people associate the company with Spot-So-Long, Spotso also makes three or four less successful products. In fact, the company is having a flat year in spite of record sales of Spot-So-Long.

Spotso needs to cut costs. In looking for ways to do so, you examine your distribution costs. You could cut your shipping costs considerably if you could use eighteen-wheel rigs instead of the smaller ten-wheel trucks you have been using. It becomes clear that ordinances restricting the weight of trucks on town streets are a problem. What's needed is a variance, just for the three streets these trucks have to use to get from the town limits to your loading dock.

A variance to allow heavier-weight truck passage requires a public hearing. You consider that a mere formality. Customer loyalty to Spot-So-Long shows that people must like Spotso; more people in town use Spot-So-Long than any other brand. Still, perhaps you should test the water to see just how much support you have in the community. You send a vice president to get some market research. He goes downtown to ask passersby a simple question.

"Is Spotso a good company?"

A woman whose husband works for Spotso says "Yes." Spotso keeps food on the table and pays for the filling of her son's countless cavities.

A man who just paid his property taxes says "Yes." Spotso's contribution to the local tax base helps keep taxes low.

A boy who plays on a Little League team says "Yes." Spotso donated enough money to the team for new uniforms.

A town councilwoman says "Yes," because Spotso does all of these things.

Spotso is a good company!

But wait. Not so fast. A local environmentalist says "No." Spotso dumps phosphates into the local river, and now the algae is so thick you can walk across in golf shoes.

A woman who invested in Spotso stock options says "No." She lost a bundle because Spotso's profits were down 24 percent and the company's share price dropped six points.

A union member says "No." Spotso laid off 10 percent of its workers and demanded concessions from the rest.

A man whose wife died in an accident says "No," because Spotso declined to contribute $100,000 toward a new trauma center at the hospital.

Spotso is a bad company!

We're oversimplifying, but the principle is valid: Your spot cleaner may be irresistible, but the perceived quality of your company and its management may have little to do with cleaning products. This is not to say that corporate image and product quality are unrelated—they are intimately related, and your marketing communications should reflect that. By definition, they're one part of your corporate impact you really want people to see and accept. If only people would just forget about your CFO's conviction for wire fraud and remember how sensational your spot remover is.

Yet traditional product publicity often relies heavily on the "halo" effect of corporate impact. That is, "good companies" make "good products," and thus it follows that "good products" must come from "good companies."

Here is the inevitable exception to the rule:

Which of these laundry detergents is made by Procter & Gamble (P&G)?

- Dash
- Tide
- Cheer
- Bold 3
- Ivory
- Era

If you picked Tide, you were right!

Of course, if you picked any of them you would have been equally correct. Master marketer P&G long ago realized that if products didn't prominently display the company's name, there could be more than one P&G product in a given category without consumers smelling a rat. And, better yet, if consumers had some predisposition against one brand, say, Bold 3, they would not necessarily shun another Procter & Gamble product. Colgate Palmolive plays in the same league, but its products do include Colgate toothpaste and Palmolive detergent. Nowhere will you see Procter paste or Gamble soap.

One could surmise, then, that corporate visibility is a low priority for P&G. It would be convenient at this point to be able to say that this strategy has created a real problem for P&G. Actually, the reverse is true. The company has realized a direct benefit from divorcing the corporate and product identities. Several years ago, an unknown soul (suspected but never proven to be a competitor) began spreading the word that P&G's century-old man-in-the-moon logo was a diabolical symbol, proof that P&G was run by servants of the devil. This weird proposition played surprisingly well in the Bible belt, where boycotts of P&G products began to be organized with support from some church groups. Only the most dedicated activists checked for the extremely fine print that identified Tide as a P&G product. But they helpfully distributed lists of P&G products to make sure the connection with the parent company was not missed. Over several years, this spurious satanic contention began to gain fairly widespread momentum, and eventually the company was forced to swallow its pride and alter its logo, making it virtually invisible on its containers.

So, although there was a benefit to separating the corporation from its products, the episode supports our earlier contention that product quality and corporate image are interrelated. P&G apparently viewed the connection for the most part as a negative. When the corporate symbol became tainted and the connection adversely affected P&G sales, the company de-emphasized the logo, and the problem subsided. For P&G, the dominant correlation in the consumer's mind was between "bad companies" and "bad products."

Most companies act on the assumption, as noted earlier, that the more important correlation is between "good companies" and "good products." Enhancing the corporate image is an accepted technique for developing and maintaining market share as the good-company products pave the way for new ones to be launched.

Previously, we mentioned that many companies rely on sponsorship of events or support of popular causes to convince consumers they are "good" companies, and thus purvey superior products—a completely irrational, yet almost universally successful marketing strategy. Several years ago, Ford Motor Company sponsored a nationwide annual competition in which boys vied to see who could throw a football farthest. The "Punt, Pass and Kick" promotion was as well known in seventh-grade gym classes as tollhouse cookies were in seventh-grade Home-Ec classes. Thousands of would-be pros diligently punted, passed, and kicked away for regional recognition and a brief moment in the limelight. A small handful achieved their dream of competing in the finals on live television during the halftime of a pro football game.

We are not aware of how many Ford automobiles were sold as a direct result of the promotion, but answer this: If you think the car you bought last year is a lemon, would you feel better about it because the company that built it underwrites a place-kicking contest each year for schoolboys? Maybe not, but then you might feel differently if

Chapter 1

your son were one of the local or regional winners, or if you
hailed Ford for providing youngsters with an outlet for
good, clean fun instead of drug abuse, premarital sex,
graffiti, and other societal ills of the day. You might even
give the car dealer one more chance to fix the transmis-
sion.

The technique also can be found working in reverse: Good
products certainly enhance the image of a company.
Consider any product you personally rate tops in quality
and value—it's almost a sure bet that you have a positive
(or at worst, a high neutral) disposition toward the manufacturer. For instance, much of this book was written
using WordPerfect word processing software. We don't
know anyone at WordPerfect, and the company's management may be one step ahead of the Justice Department for
all we know, but we think the product is one of God's
smaller miracles and will always have a warm spot for
anyone associated with it.

Does this phenomenon have a flipside? Ask Dow Chemical, the company that, according to recent advertising,
"lets you do great things." Back in the sixties, word got
around that those great things primarily consisted of
making great napalm and Agent Orange. Dow, then and
today, insisted that the company only made the chemicals—the *government* spewed the napalm and sprayed the
defoliant up and down Vietnam. Be that as it may, a
generation of Americans still holds Dow up as the para-
digm of venality.

The result was a swearing off of Dow products by millions
of young people (some of whom then were able to brow-

beat their parents into submission). Even today, Dow Chemical feels the effects. When the press reported that high levels of dioxin had been detected in and around Midland, Michigan, home of Dow's headquarters, many citizens around the country were less than sympathetic. Nothing was too unfortunate for the company that invented napalm. No one remembered that Dow also makes several lifesaving drugs.

The point is that the perception of product or service quality and the perception of your corporate image are related; each suffers a downturn at the expense of the other. But, in a larger sense, the overall behavior of your company—the actions of each employee, the quality of your products and services, the environmental consequences of your manufacturing processes, your labor practices, and charitable contributions, the landscaping of your plant sites, and the institutional behaviors that reveal the real you—those little (and big) disparities in life (such as the "Friendly Neighborhood Bakery, Int'l" worldwide headquarters building with the armed guards and snarling Dobermans on perimeter patrol)—all of these have some impact on public opinion. In fact, it is your "Corporate Impact."

NEWTON WAS RIGHT

Proposition 1: Organizational behavior is motivated by the desire to preserve the status quo.

Proposition 2: Human behavior is motivated by the desire to change the status quo.

Inflammatory Conclusion: Conflict is inevitable.

We use the label "inflammatory" because the conclusion and the propositions upon which it is based are the subjects of endless debate among students of such sciences as sociology, psychology, anthropology, and biology, not to mention organizational dynamics, management science, and Business Administration 101. Since we don't want to get in the middle of it all, we'll acknowledge that many people violently disagree with our thinking and invite them to include a section on public relations in their next submission to *Scientific American*.

Conflict is simply a divergence of interests. The nation's environmental laws (which rank among the most stringent in the world) are influenced by conflicting forces: Corporations need to be profitable, but not at the expense of public welfare. At the same time, the public deserves to live without fear of exposure to carcinogens, yet depends on the corporation for jobs, and has grown dependent on the corporation's products. The challenge is to strike a balance that is sufficiently responsive to the needs of the public and the corporation so that relative harmony reigns.

Managing corporate impact is all about managing conflicts. Of course, they're not all as obvious as those resulting from your environmental policies. They range from your contributions policy to more substantial issues (i.e., quality control procedures or employment policies) that cut right to the heart of your business. They can be internal or external. Precisely how you handle these issues can have substantial implications for your various audiences. Failure to anticipate these implications, knowingly or not, carries its own consequences.

All high school physics students learn Newton's Third Law of Motion: Every action has an equal and opposite reaction. Such is the relationship between a company and the public, although the reactions may not be easy to quantify individually. Over time and in the aggregate, they contribute to an altering of your corporate image, either for better or for worse. Allow your company to be seen as unethical, unapproachable, and high-handed and you'll be treated that way. We're talking about your "real" corporate image—that visceral classification of your company as, simply, good or bad—which so often influences everything from this year's bottom line to how company management will fare in a proxy contest for control.

Managing corporate impact need be neither difficult nor expensive. Ignoring it is a lot easier, but can be very, very costly—ultimately, it can cost you your corporate existence. The choice is yours.

WHAT IS PUBLIC RELATIONS, ANYWAY?

Talking about public opinion is one thing. Doing something about it is quite another. That's where public relations comes in. As we see it, public relations is the art and science of creating, altering, strengthening, or overcoming public opinion.

If our definition sounds simplistic, that's because more specific definitions are bound to get us in trouble. Depending upon whom you poll, the compiled definitions might turn into a book all by itself.

In putting this tome together, we decided to steer clear of the hoary controversy within the public relations community as to what should or should not be included in the term. We take a very liberal view of the matter in saying: Any communication of any kind that emanates from a company is relating something to some element of the public, which makes it public relations. Any problem that is susceptible to solution through any form of communications, be it publicity, sales promotion, stimulated rumor, skywriting, or practiced body language, is eligible for inclusion.

We even consider advertising a subdiscipline of public relations, albeit a highly specialized one (an aggressive statement that will surely send shivers up and down Madison Avenue). In a nutshell, as public relations professionals, we want to poke around in whatever a company is communicating because any corporate communication contributes to the overall corporate image, and corporate image is our game.

This book, however, is not a study of "how to do public relations." That text has been written many times. Rather, our purpose is to help business executives who are not professional communicators understand what constitutes an effective and responsible communications program. They will not personally manage such a program, but as more informed users of public relations services they can help solve corporate problems or prevent them from developing. In either case, whether participating in the strategic process or evaluating the result, it is critical to understand that communication does not begin with a press release and end with a thirty-second spot in prime time. What a company does is far more important than what it says about what it does because there is an army of watchers waiting to see if (in their opinion) the game the company plays measures up to the game it talks.

2

Keeping in Touch

Making the Right Impact at the Right Time on Your Audience

Corporate impact is not a difficult concept. It is the cumulative effect of the simple fact of your company's existence. A more substantive question would be, "Effect on whom?" since understanding that is the first step toward managing corporate impact.

If you picture the world as a matrix of audiences, corporate impact equals the degree and frequency with which each audience is affected by the actions you and your company take in the course of business.

A typical matrix might have the following audiences listed on one side:

- company management
- employees (unions)
- suppliers
- customers
- financial/investment community
- local community
- local/state/federal officials

Think of these audiences as "stakeholders" in your business. Each has an interest in how you run your business and, consequently, how and when you communicate with them.

On the top of the matrix might be several types of communications, including:

- quarterly financial results
- layoffs/plant closing
- new product introduction

- hostile takeover
- charitable contributions

If an "x" is placed in each box where a specific audience intersects with a type of message, the results may be surprising. For example, quarterly financial results are of obvious interest to the financial/investment community—analysts, bankers, or institutional and individual investors. Obviously, the same information is important to company management, since their business strategy is guided by the success (or failure) of their actions in the recent past.

Employees, while not as interested perhaps in the minute detail of the quarterly statements as analysts, are obviously interested in how the company is doing in general. Suppliers, who depend on your company for their own livelihood (and who may be extending a good deal of credit to you) have an interest in the health of the company. The local community, including families of employees, local restaurants, office supply firms, and the like, has a deep concern for the financial stability of the company, as do local officials who rely on your company for employment and tax revenue.

A new product introduction may be of equal interest to the global audience, or may have narrower effects. For instance, a new kitchen gadget will be of greater general interest than a new industrial lathe. Even so, news about the product will be of interest to a wider audience than one might think at first, since the success or failure of the new product can have dramatic implications for all. The introduction of a new passenger jet, for example, represents a huge financial commitment on the part of Boeing or McDonnell Douglas—if the plane is a financial success, all audiences benefit. If the plane never takes off, so to speak, all audiences are hurt.

This overall impact may seem a rather basic concept, yet the frequency with which it is ignored or suppressed is surprising. There are any number of reasons why companies fail to take all audiences into account; for one thing, ours is a fast-paced society and simply taking the time to analyze the overall impact of a business decision may be precluded by short-term expediency.

Another reason is that many managers simply do not understand who their audiences really are. Impact can be complicated.

Many of the audiences listed in the matrix can be broken down into subcategories. For example, the financial community can be separated into bankers, brokers, analysts, and investors. Analysts can be either sell–side (retail) or buy–side (institutional). Investors can be institutional or individual.

Each of these subcategories can be listed on a matrix, and each may ascribe a particular significance to specific developments at your company. Each may seem interested only in the narrow area of your company that intersects with their constituency. If you announce that your company is undertaking a major purchase of Japanese-made components, sell–side analysts might be pleased because you saved a huge amount of money (improving the bottom line) while institutional investors, sensitive to the concerns of the labor union pension funds they often manage, might be annoyed enough that you didn't "buy American" to dump your stock altogether.

Just as the overall audience grid should be considered when assessing the impact of a given development or decision, each audience can be targeted separately to achieve a desired end. Often, they *must* be, to ensure that your message is received. A lone press release or advertisement cannot reach everyone—obviously, not every publication will use the release, and not everyone reads every publication or watches television when your ad runs.

THE PEN IS MIGHTIER THAN THE ANTI-AIRCRAFT GUN

With all of this targeting going on, we should spend a moment examining the affectionately applied term "flak" as a reference to public relations people. Our dictionary says that the origin of the term as used in this connection is "unknown." We have our own theory.

One of the authors was born after World War II, and one . . . was not. The latter remembers that flak is an antiquated term referring to fragments of exploding shells that were sent aloft into the night skies over Berlin to down Allied bombers during WWII. Flak eliminated the need for dead-eye accuracy—send up enough of it and you were bound to hit something.

Such is the image many business people still have of the media relations process: Send out enough press releases to enough publications and you're bound to get some coverage. Hence, the term flak joins the long list of nicknames given to professionals, including "mouthpiece," "bean-counter," and "sawbones."

These days, flak is considered obsolete as a defensive weapon; it was made so by the advent of such weapons as surface-to-air and Sidewinder missiles. The flak analogy applied to media relations is equally obsolete.

The quantity of press clippings generated can be a legitimate means of assessing breadth of coverage, which can be important for a new product introduction. But often, a much narrower distribution of press materials is needed. Sometimes only a relative handful of people need to be reached at a given moment, and press relations is but one means of reaching target audiences.

IT'S NOT WHO YOU KNOW, IT'S WHAT'S NEW

While we're on the subject of press relations, we should mention the energy expended trying to maintain contacts at major publications. There is a misconception as to why these contacts are so useful. The hasty conclusion is that contacts help publicists "plant" stories, presumably to get stories into a publication that would not otherwise see the light of day. Most reputable practitioners agree it is difficult to place a nonstory, and trying too hard to do so only decreases the likelihood that a reporter will answer one's phone calls next time. Good press contacts may be helpful with a marginal story because the editor knows he or she can expect help from the source in developing the piece and so may be willing to take a chance on it. But the greatest advantage gained by good press contact is learning what plans the publication has for upcoming features. Sometimes you may be able to work your company's story into the overall piece.

Communications vehicles have to be chosen according to the audience you need to reach. They can include press releases, advertising, seminars, speeches, personal meetings, letters, telephone calls—each audience has its own preferred means of giving and receiving information.

That is important because communications may need to be tightly focused on one or two of these audiences, in special circumstances. It's not uncommon for a desired outcome to depend on the actions of one key decision maker.

For example, suppose your company manufactures a new and improved blood gas analyzer. Let's say it is more expensive than the current industry standard but processes samples 40 percent faster and is 80 percent more accurate.

Patients don't buy these contraptions, so an "I Am Joe's Thyroid" piece in *Reader's Digest* isn't going to set the world on fire for you. Obviously, a favorable reference in *Medical Electronics* would be of far greater benefit. A favorable review in *Hospital Purchasing* might be even more effective: Health care institutions are just as motivated by cost as by efficacy, and the purchasing agent may have as much or more decision-making power than a physician.

That's why identifying the audiences you need to reach to accomplish your objective and determining the messages you need to convey to them amount to more than half the battle—they have become (in a way) the "science" of public relations and perhaps the biggest single challenge you face in managing your corporate impact.

Chapter 2

The "art" is in determining the best way to reach those audiences. Sometimes, after considerable analysis, you might determine that the media are the wrong forum altogether. Suppose your company is a defense contractor competing with several other firms for the contract to provide #10 washers for military vehicles. The company may be doing pretty well, and (assuming it is a public company) may be the darling of Wall Street, but securing that contract hangs on convincing the decision maker (perhaps a congressman or a functionary at the Department of Defense). A nice profile in the local paper isn't going to get that contract. The decision maker needs to be convinced that your washer is the best for the job. He needs to be able to document that the washer is the least expensive, that you can deliver on schedule, and, ultimately, that his decision won't become a scandal—a "Washergate."

In this case, publicity alone probably won't win the day. You need a lobbyist who can demonstrate the wisdom of selecting your washer. The best lobbyists can accomplish a great deal in a fraction of the time it might otherwise take you. If your timing is right, you might be able to incite the calling of a public congressional hearing on washer selection.

But even if you have retained an effective lobbyist, press relations can still make a major contribution to the cause. A well-timed article in a defense industry publication that refers positively to your washer (for instance, mercenaries in Angola have experienced a much lower replacement rate than with a competitor's washer) can help support the lobbyist's efforts by providing that all-important third-party endorsement. A favorable piece in the *National*

Journal or the *Washington Post* decrying the waste of taxpayer dollars on $14 washers can help even more. Of questionable value would be a *Town and Country* profile of the company president that pictures him around his stables.

Seems pretty basic, doesn't it? Just as one segments markets, one should also segment the media that reach those markets.

Reaching the desired media has become more complicated in recent years because they (particularly the print media) have become increasingly esoteric. There seems to be a magazine, for example, for practically every line of work. To manage the impact of your communications, you have to know what audience is routinely reached by a specific publication, and what publications are routinely read by the audience you're trying to reach.

While "contacts" at major media—the *New York Times, Wall Street Journal, Business Week*—are still as valuable as ever, it is almost impossible to keep up with personnel changes at some of the highly targeted trade or industry publications. In addition, new publications are springing up all the time. Ultimately, with trade magazines or major daily newspapers, a good story is the best tool; you don't have to be pals with a reporter or editor to place it.

Consider the *New York Times*. What is its primary mission? To inform? To entertain? To influence governmental policy? To line the bottoms of canary cages? The answer is, "None of the above." While the *Times* undoubtedly does all of these things and more, its primary goal is the same as your company's: to make money for its owners, the shareholders. The 35 cents one pays for a copy barely covers the cost of printing and distribution, so the *Times* accomplishes its basic goal by selling advertising space.

Advertisers use the *Times* because a lot of people read it each day. The more people read the *Times*, the more the *Times* can charge for advertising space. So, it behooves the *Times* to print stuff that people want to read. Yes, yes, very basic.

The editors of the *Times* have deduced that what people want to read is information that enlightens and/or entertains. If your press release enables the *Times* to provide that service to its readers, it will be well received. If not, it will be discarded. Simple as that. It *can* be made more complicated; you can sometimes impose on friendships you have developed with reporters to cover (or not cover) a story, but they won't stay friends for long.

Press relations is an important tool in managing your impact because the media are often the most efficient channel for reaching your target audiences. Yet, don't lose sight of other ways in which you can get your message across: direct mail, advertising, speeches, and seminars also can be effective.

... AND IN ALL THINGS, CONSISTENCY

Regardless of the vehicle, message consistency is the key—pick a theme and stick with it, no matter what vehicle you use to communicate. You can vary it to suit specific audiences, as long as you don't end up sending conflicting messages to different audiences.

The most common faux pas is usually found right at home. Your own employees (who are more aware than you think they are) will be quick to note when you are talking a better game than you play.

Despite the fact that little happens in a business without employee cooperation, companies continually forget that those employees read the papers, too. What a company says to the outside world can have a major impact on employee morale. For example, when a company files for Chapter 11 protection, employees are understandably upset. They assume that the company is obviously in dire straits and that their jobs may be eliminated.

However, at least two huge corporations—Texaco and Johns Manville—have filed for Chapter 11 protection for strategic reasons other than the actual fiscal condition of the companies. No large-scale layoffs occurred; in fact, both companies "thrived in bankruptcy." The business management community usually understands what's going on, but employees (especially at nonmanagement levels of the company) may only see the mortgage or car payments they won't be able to meet if they are laid off. Unless an effort is made to reassure them immediately, employee morale may plummet. Uncertainty breeds fear and insecurity. Also, as often happens when companies are takeover victims, some workers may develop stress-related disorders. Drug and alcohol abuse may increase, with resultant absenteeism. Employees may find jobs elsewhere.

Productivity improvement also demands credible employee communications. Most companies' strategic plans include some communications component, primarily directed outside the company. In the rush to let outside audiences know how aggressive and market-driven it is, a company often overlooks the fact that the success of the plan depends on the abilities and willingness of employees to change the way they do what they do, or even to do something else entirely.

Some companies have the right idea, but bungle the implementation. One of the more atrocious instances was provided by the senior management of a major New York City life insurance company. It is a perfect example of coupling a worthy concept with an unfortunate (even bizarre) implementation.

The company's management had concluded that its target audiences saw the company as sluggish and conservative. What was needed was a way to document the insurer's creativity and market sensitivity. Clients (pension fund managers, for instance) needed to see that the company prized creativity and initiative at all levels, and provided an environment in which any employee could feel comfortable being creative.

Since, as the company understood, the success of such an undertaking hinged on employee receptivity, the first requirement was to get each employee enthused and "on board." So far, so good. One can hardly expect the outside world to accept as gospel what one's own employees think is bogus. The actions of each employee would support or belie the company's contention that it was attuned to the needs of its clients, so it made sense to target a special communications effort at employees.

The company moved boldly.

On a frosty winter's day, employees who frequented the company's cafeteria were perplexed by a large banner hung on the wall. It read simply "WDTG."

Luncheon conversation briefly centered on what WDTG might mean, but no one took much notice until a few days later, when the banner was replaced by a huge calendar. On it, a day later in the month was called WDTG day, and circled in red.

Speculation began to mount. What could WDTG mean? Soon, the cafeteria featured a daily special including foods that began with the letters W, D, T, and G. Curiosity was further sparked.

Rumors began to circulate as to the meaning of WDTG. Perhaps the most popular concerned a recent development at a major competitor, where employees had been given an across-the-board percentage of salary as bonus compensation for a great year. Could it be that WDTG stood for "We'll Double Their Generosity?"

One thing was certain—despite the natural tendency in corporations for information leaks to develop, in this instance none had. Only three or four people at the most senior level of management knew for sure the meaning of the cryptic initials. And they were not telling—not yet.

As the day, WDTG day, neared, employees began comparing notes on how each would spend the bonus. Some had already made purchases in anticipation of the found money. Even those who would normally cast a jaundiced eye toward such a manipulative exercise were becoming enthused.

Finally after nearly a month of waiting, employees went home on a Friday night knowing that Monday would be the big day. The weekend was almost unbearable.

Monday brought with it a blizzard. Normally, such bad weather is accompanied by large-scale absences. Not this day. Not WDTG day. Employees braved the snow and icy roads, the delayed trains and freezing temperatures to make it to their desks on time.

Midmorning, a memo was circulated stating that the company's CEO would speak to a group of employees at noon, at last revealing the significance of WDTG. Since there was no facility within the building large enough to accommodate all employees at once, the memo requested each department to send one delegate. In addition, the speech would be videotaped, so that all employees could view the speech for themselves later.

Noon came slowly. At last, each department's representative hurried to the auditorium. The CEO stood up and began his speech.

It seemed that as their company had grown, people were having a hard time communicating with one another. Worse yet, he said, was the system of barriers that existed within the corporate structure. These barriers stifled creativity. An employee with a good idea was often discouraged by his or her superiors.

In order to remain competitive, he went on, the company had to dedicate itself to removing these barriers, to allow people at all levels of the company to achieve their maximum creative output. The CEO then announced that he was on this day inaugurating a program to eliminate barriers from the top of the corporation to the bottom. He outlined a series of procedural changes (fairly dry stuff) and eventually moved to the climax.

In one year's time, he proclaimed, "We'll look back to this day, the day that barriers started to come down. We'll look back at those barriers and we'll wonder 'Where Did They Go?'" Get it? WDTG, *Where Did They Go*.

The CEO thanked the employees for their attention, and concluded the meeting to thunderous silence.

The returning delegates were besieged upon arriving at their desks. Few could recall the full impact (such as it was) of the CEO's speech; most could only relay the "most important" part—no bonus.

Word soon got around that within six months the CEO would be able to look back at all of the angry, disappointed employees in every department and ask: "Where Did They Go?" Instead of inspiring creativity and initiative, the company had engendered great hostility among its employees, who felt belittled and betrayed.

So, employees are an important entry on the list of crucial audiences you need on your side, to accomplish the many business goals that require a shift (subtle or not) in how the world looks at you.

Are there others? Of course, but the list could grow quite long, and it's not our intention to examine each audience and demonstrate how each is affected by a particular action. (There is no "one-size-fits-all" answer, and in any case, we charge by the hour for that kind of analysis.)

What we can say with some confidence is that somewhere, someone is reacting to nearly every action your company takes—reacting in a positive or negative way. We wouldn't recommend becoming obsessed with anticipating each particular reaction, or even watching every audience continually (even if it were possible). What we would recommend is that you take time to consider, whenever you undertake a major business decision or embark upon a new strategy, the likely effect these actions will have on the audiences you want to keep happy. If you really want to play it safe, you can quietly poll a cross section of a given audience to get a sense of how the universe will react, but often that's not necessary. Common sense and your ability to step into another person's shoes for a moment will serve you well enough most of the time.

3

Hot Concepts

Positioning and Corporate Culture

Chapter 3

Two words that have had a dramatic influence on the business of public relations are "positioning" and "culture."

"Positioning" frequently seems to be coupled with "corporate," as does "culture."

First, we'll discuss corporate positioning. Someone must have had some definite concept in mind when the term corporate positioning was coined, but it's now so overused it seems to mean less than nothing anymore.

(By the way, "corporate impact" is not a buzzword; it's just a concept. Never say "corporate impact" in public. For those of you who are still into transcendental meditation, treat "corporate impact" as you would your mantra. Internalize it. If possible, only speak the term while inhaling.)

Corporate positioning connotes a relationship. When we say corporate positioning, we generally mean viewing the corporation, or causing it to be viewed by others, in relation to the position of other corporations. In part, it is the identification of your "unique selling proposition" with the emphasis on the word "unique." That uniqueness establishes a position for your company relative to another.

Since presumably everything that your company is and does contributes to its overall position, defining that position can be complex, especially if your company is in the business of supplying services rather than products (whose unique attributes form the basis of product positioning). The process of corporate positioning is neither simple nor finite. It evolves as your company evolves—the process never ends.

But that doesn't mean the basic concept is complex; the simplicity of the concept must have bothered some people, who insisted on heaping great significance on the term instead of on the process, where it belongs. Suddenly, "positioning" became a buzzword—everyone was saying it. It became the public relations equivalent of brown rice and Velcro for the Woodstock generation. Such a nugget was quickly added to the business lexicon, taking its rightful place beside "net–net," "bottom line," and the endless incarnations and reincarnations of "excellence."

Still, it's a useful term, if only as shorthand for the overall concept.

In the WDTG example, the company in question was attempting to position itself as market driven and nurturing of employee initiative and creativity. By extension (it was hoped), the competition would be perceived as less market driven and less nurturing, if not arrogant and stodgy.

Putting aside the abysmal execution of the WDTG strategy, the concept itself made sense. In the world of insurance (and most financial services) proprietary products remain proprietary for about three weeks. As soon as a new brochure can be slapped on a printing press, the competition is offering essentially the same product.

What separates one firm from another, then, isn't the

products but the delivery system and service mechanism backing them. If the target consumer perceives that a company offers better or more attentive or more personal or faster or easier access to the product, relative pricing may be secondary.

So, positioning the company as, say, "in touch with customer needs," or "the company that cares about you" may then be legitimate—if it's true.

This, of course, brings us to corporate culture. Corporate culture is nearly perfectly analogous to national or ethnic culture. It is what we, of shared experience and commonality (in this case, the same employer), believe in and hence, how we do things. Corporate culture evolves from the heroes of the company; from the company's accomplishments as an organization and its importance to our society; and from how it treats its people and how its leaders are viewed by the world.

As people have come to recognize that all companies have some kind of culture (some are more defined than others—the "IBM Way" or the "GE Style" have become almost palpable over the years), the term has grown so popular and is so bandied about that it is now nearly devoid of meaning, which is too bad. It, too, is a concept worth understanding, especially since many business problems can be traced to the gap between expectations and realities of the existing corporate culture.

It is more than just a dreadful pun to say that behind many unhealthy cultures lies a staff infection. The corporate culture is driven from the top of an organization down, but its efficacy is measured from the bottom up. The behavior of all employees reflects the true culture of a company, not the mission statement. When the WDTG fiasco was conceived, it made perfect sense to the CEO. Where the fatal error was made was in the implementation, which assumed that the concept was compatible with the existing culture. Obviously, it was not. Even if the kickoff had been a triumph, the strategy would just as likely have failed. It asked for too much too soon.

If barriers are to come down, the existing chain of communication has to be disrupted. That might seem like a great idea to the CEO, but not so hot to the middle manager who wants to preserve the status quo. Would you want a subordinate to go over your head with a great idea? Would you not then be perceived as the barrier the company was trying to jettison?

That doesn't mean the idea is a bad one. To implement it simply will require a change in culture—and that process is a long-term one. To effect even a fine tuning of a culture can take many months. A complete redirection can take as long as five years from conception to realization, and even then, some old (and young) dogs just won't learn new tricks.

In the WDTG case, the management attempted to change in the span of a month a culture that had evolved over many decades. Evolution was pitted against spontaneous mutation, and the would-be mutants mutinied.

How would you avoid such an unpleasant outcome? The answer centers on research.

POSITIONING BEGINS WITH RESEARCH

The basis for corporate positioning is an understanding of where your company is—that is, how it is now perceived—and where you would like it to be. Too many companies begin and end with the latter perspective, as if admitting where the firm is today is somehow self-deprecating. Yet how would you drive to Omaha if you didn't know whether you were in Los Angeles or New York? How can you set a positioning goal without knowing how you are positioned today?

That's exactly what the well-intentioned insurance executives who begot the WDTG debacle did. They figured out what the marketplace wanted the ideal financial services company to be and set out to become it. The evidence shows that they skipped over the first, and equally important, step.

Assessing Where You Are

"Research" is a word that puts off many executives, who see it as expensive, complicated, and ultimately unproductive. A research project can be all of those things if it is researching the wrong things, or if it is undertaken for the wrong reasons.

Properly designed and conducted, though, research can be an immensely valuable tool in the positioning process, especially *qualitative* research. However, *quantitative* research—how many, how much, how often—has its place also, particularly in developing a marketing strategy. This usually involves surveying a relatively large sample of people to allow the drawing of reasonably accurate conclusions about the population as a whole. Such research is best undertaken by professionals, and is usually pretty expensive. (Researchers correctly note that embarking on a strategy based on faulty, often visceral criteria can be even more costly.)

But qualitative research may involve as few as fifteen or twenty telephone calls or visits. If you select the interviewees carefully, their responses will be enough to establish a baseline from which to develop your positioning goal.

The fact that such research is neither terribly expensive nor complicated does not mean that it is best done internally. The people being interviewed will speak more candidly if a third party is involved. Usually, the third party promises that the interviewees' responses will be confidential, which helps stimulate more honest responses. At the same time, your company's identity is also protected, usually by the interviewer asking questions about several competitors (which also helps place the interviewees' comments about your company in perspective).

Often, the people interviewed are reporters, because how they perceive your company influences what they write about it. Reporters who perceive your company in a certain way can influence many thousands of consumers who read their stories. Existing and potential customers can be interviewed as well, especially when your company supplies extremely expensive or technical equipment. Your universe of potential customers decreases dramatically in such a case, and a smaller sample will be more

representative of the whole than, say, interviewing twenty
users of ballpoint pens.

The interviewer, armed with perhaps twenty questions,
tries to stimulate a discussion with the people being
interviewed: A simple yes or no will not suffice. You need
to know not just how people feel but why, and how they
feel regarding the competition. You might ask also if the
person ever thinks of your company as possessing desirable attributes (i.e., "Would you say that XYZ Company is
market driven?").

What you should end up with is a composite picture of
how your company is perceived by audiences who are
important to you. That's pretty valuable information.
Usually it is also pretty depressing because for the first
time you can see just how much work you have ahead of
you.

Assessing Where You Want to Be

The information you glean from research is most valuable
when it gives you a strategic direction to follow in your
marketing plans. Often, the person interviewed will speak
in terms of your company as opposed to another, citing
examples (positive or negative) of key differences. If the
competition has legitimate, positive attributes that make
it stand out from yours, you then have a role model to
emulate and hopefully surpass.

Frequently, customer research is one of the best ways to
improve your products or services. If numerous customers
complain, for example, about the difficulty they experi-

enced getting technical support or servicing for your products, you may want to give some thought to reorganizing your customer service mechanism. With luck, customers will notice the difference right away, but you can get additional mileage out of such improvements through direct mail to your customer base, and through the trade press. A company that listens to customers and makes helpful changes always makes good copy; it's so unusual. (As we write these words, the good folks at General Foods, makers of Post Raisin Bran, have started using "ZIP· PAK" bags inside their cardboard boxes to allow consumers to reseal the inner package and preserve freshness. Emblazoned across the box are the words: "You Talked—Post Listened!" The company's raisin bran has graced American breakfast tables for at least three decades, and for as long as we can remember, the cereal always came in waxed paper bags (inside the boxes) that tore apart upon first being opened and sent cereal in all directions. That is until now, when "we" finally got Post's attention. The box should read, "You Talked—Post Finally Listened." Or more likely, "Dow Talked—Post Listened," to reflect the joint promotion that appears to have led to the new packaging.)

Another benefit of research can be to point up the divergence between your perception of your company and that of your target audiences. You may find that you have unrealistic expectations about how you would like to be seen in a given period of time.

We once met with a prospective client who had heard the agency had done some interesting work with high-tech products. His company sold, he told us, a revolutionary product: a high-tech toilet. As we later learned, he considered the product high-tech because it was made of some miracle plastic that had never been put to such a use before, and it used less water than standard toilets. What's more, he rather fancied himself the president of a high-tech company.

But his only product, after all, was still a toilet, and as such had not been revolutionary since indoor plumbing became the norm. In the public mind, toilets had a long way to go before they could be thought of as "high-tech." No one, especially the venture capitalists he was hoping to impress through public relations, would be likely to think of his company as "leading edge"—not now, not five years from now. Undertaking research wasn't necessary to figure that out.

Employee Research

Don't forget to include a survey of your employees. As we saw in the WDTG example, just because you say your company is innovative doesn't make it so, and as noted, they have to be convinced first. Your employees may have a quite different set of criteria for deciding how innovative your company is, and it is important for them to understand why you feel the way you do. They'll also be more than vaguely curious about how you intend to engineer the transition, especially if it means they'll be learning new procedures or even new skills.

It can be amazing how differently people in your company see your company. One client surveyed its employees, asking just one question: What is your most important responsibility at work? Answers ranged from "Coming to work" to "Making the employees happy." Not one of dozens of returned forms mentioned "Making customers happy" or, for that matter, "Making money for the company." This was not a market driven company we're talking about, and it would have been foolish, in light of the responses, to hope customers would see it as such. You can't ignore how your audiences see you, just as you can't ignore how they see themselves.

4

Do Unto Others

Why Consumerism Should
Guide Your Business

Consumerism is one of those terms that has mysteriously shifted in its connotation over the years. If we were to ask for a definition of consumerism, most people would suggest that it refers to consumer awareness: making sure that the consumer doesn't fall prey to an unscrupulous corporation.

In fact, when the term was coined, consumerism referred to the concern a company displayed for the interests of its consumers. If the first definition is the same as "let the buyer beware," then the second, original definition equals The Golden Rule.

History is on the side of the latter interpretation. Since the creation of the Federal Trade Commission (FTC) in 1914, the federal government has taken the position that individuals are largely powerless to defend themselves against the venality of the corporation. If the corporation won't display concern for the consumer voluntarily, then the government will force it to do so.

We're talking extremes here. The FTC is concerned with such matters as specious advertising claims and other unsavory practices that betray a willful disregard for the general welfare. Maybe you're not guilty of such behavior, but that alone doesn't make you a paragon of consumerism.

Consumerism can (and should) be a guiding force in the management of your business, if we define it as the process of identifying and addressing the concerns of one's consumers. In that sense, consumerism is at the heart of managing corporate impact.

Too often, corporations exhibit "after-the-fact" consumerism—mouthing concern for the consumer's interests only after those interests have been violated and an immediate need for remedial action springs up. Sometimes corporations knowingly proceed in direct conflict with the interests of the consumer, with disastrous results (the Ford Pinto debacle comes to mind).

Consumerism is proactive, not reactive. It is an extension of the bond of trust that develops between the consumer and the purveyor—trust that the product or service purchased will do what it is supposed to do without unanticipated negative developments.

Consumers trust that they will feel better if they take your pills.

They trust that your cars will go when they start them and stop when they hit the brakes.

They trust that when they deposit money in your bank, they'll be able to get it back when they want it.

They trust that your manufacturing process is not polluting the water they drink.

Most of all, they trust that if your wares have not lived up to their expectations, you will make good on their complaint (although their credulity has been strained in recent years).

Consumerism means looking at your products or services from the perspective of the consumer and making sure that they will fulfill reasonable expectations.

Presumably, if your business has been successful, you have been practicing consumerism to some degree, at least with customers. But you can apply consumerism tactics to your dealings with employees, shareholders, suppliers, community leaders, and all of your other stakeholders, including the media. For example, in the latter instance, consumerism would dictate that you be forthcoming and candid in your dealings with the press; that you be as open about bad news as you are about good; that a press conference will reveal something newsworthy; and that you respect a reporter's integrity and responsibility to report as objectively and fairly as possible.

That said, we note that the more current definition of consumerism—behavior exhibited by consumers—has implications for your company, too. People *are* more wary than they used to be and less inclined to accept what you say as entirely credible. In part, that's due to the realization that companies haven't always acted in the interest of the consumer, and in some cases (the Pinto again) have actually acted with apparent reckless disregard for their customers. Medicines have been known to produce ghastly side effects; certain cars have had a reputation for lurching forward or in reverse independent of the driver; banks have gone under in recent years at an alarming rate; and as we approach the nineties, Americans can no longer look upon a steady supply of untainted water as a birthright. These examples do not necessarily suggest that the corporations involved are motivated by evil, but neither do they seem to imply that these corporations are motivated by consumerism.

Consumerism as popularly defined brings with it the notion of accountability. If consumers have serious complaints about the quality of a product or service and can't get satisfaction from the seller or manufacturer, they can sue. What's more, the chances are good that they will sue. If enough people raise the issue, a government agency may get involved, to put it mildly. (In some cases, the government may identify a potential problem initially, and then consumers sue.)

In growing numbers, corporations are being held accountable for their actions—recent actions and those of decades past. Nowhere is this trend more in evidence than in the area of environmental issues; as often as not, the presumption of accountability outweighs the presumption of innocence, precipitating a crisis.

Consumerism is probably the single most important contributor to the need to manage corporate impact because increasingly, consumers are redefining what it means to be a consumer. With society telling us that we should all be consumer advocates in our own behalf, we are cognizant of the need to do more than kick the tires when we buy a car. Thanks to the proliferation of publications such as *Motor Trend* and *Consumer Reports*, making an informed choice is easier than ever.

With environmental matters, it's not so easy. As consumers of air and water, we are becoming more and more concerned about what corporations are dumping into the environment. Traditionally, we have had to rely on government experts to protect our interests. That was until the inclusion of the Community Right To Know (CRTK) section into the revised Superfund Act (dealt with in greater detail in a later chapter). CRTK is simple in its intent: to coerce corporations to "clean up their act" through public pressure and nothing more. The Act now assumes that as consumers we can make our own judgments about what constitutes a hazard and then force corporations to take remedial action. Whether that is a well-founded conclusion is irrelevant: It is the law, and companies that handle hazardous substances have entered a whole new era in community relations because of it.

California's Proposition 65, which not only assumes that the public can make intelligent analyses of chemical hazards in the community but contains a "bounty hunter" fine-sharing arrangement to encourage whistle-blowing, was passed by a wide majority of the state's voters.

In this tempestuous communications environment, opportunities to stand out as a leader are as widespread as the chances to self-destruct. In March 1988, after years of discussion as to whether the ozone layer was being adversely affected by the use of chlorofluorocarbons (CFCs), Du Pont, the maker of more than 25 percent of the total world production of CFCs, announced that it would phase out all CFC production by the turn of the century. In so doing, Du Pont will have raised the standards by which corporate responsibility—and true consumerism—are measured.

No matter how well-managed your company is, if it's a juicy target, someone will take a shot at it. The shooting may come even if you have been a model of consumerism. But, if you have worked at keeping your key audiences' needs in mind in the normal course of business, you'll have a lot better chance of attracting supporters to your side when the apocalypse comes knocking at your door.

5

Corporate Visibility

How to Focus the Glare

Chapter 5

In the normal course of affairs, even the best managed communications program is driven by internal and external forces that may be, at times, in competition with each other.

At one end of the spectrum is the company-initiated communication, whose sole purpose is to advance the interests of the company. A press conference to introduce a new product or service is an example. These are announcements that the company wants everyone to know about.

At the other end of the spectrum is the externally mandated communication—information a company may not be too enthusiastic about disclosing. It's probably safe to include in this category anything requested by means of a subpoena; more commonly, we're talking about the prescribed release of "material" information for the benefit or protection of shareholders.

Such disclosure is not always painful; indeed, a magnificent earnings release is something any company wants to share with anyone who will listen. Unfortunately, there are also times when a company must announce something they would just as soon keep in the family. A case of the latter would be, of course, a report of depressed earnings. Bad news about top management is another. For example, Wall Street analysts often pin their hopes for the success of start-up companies on the intellect and imagination of the founder. If the founder is incapacitated by Alzheimer's Disease, that's "material information," and shareholders have a right to know about it (or so says the Securities and Exchange Commission, and it's their ballgame).

Somewhere in the middle of these extremes is an area of overlapping interests that forms the basis of corporate impact. For example, it is in the company's interest to support the value of its stock, to encourage current stockholders to hang onto it, and to attract new stockholders. One of the most frequently used tools in this effort is the securities analysts' meeting. Here company management attempts to put forth as rosy a picture of its current and future prospects as possible in hopes that the analysts will in turn speak favorably about the company. Security analysts get to ask the tough questions that help them decide whether the stock is a buy, hold, or sell—in other words, the meeting helps the analysts be better at their job. At this point, the company's interests intersect with those of an important external audience. By extension, the process helps create and maintain value for stockholders, and everybody wins.

Somewhere in, around, and over this middle ground lies general corporate visibility: the goal of those communications activities that a company undertakes to enhance its overall image. The corporation assumes that such enhancement can both benefit the sale of products (though the company's products may scarcely be mentioned in the process) and communicate to external audiences (without a targeted effort) specific information about the company in a way that ultimately benefits the company.

There are several reasons why companies seek to increase their corporate visibility. For one thing, although product visibility is crucial too, sometimes the corporation itself is the product being "sold." For example, you want to put the best face on the company when you are recruiting new talent. Prospective employees, especially the ones who are in demand by the competition, will consider your general reputation, along with the compensation package, in making their decision.

A strong and favorable corporate image can ease the process of mergers and acquisitions—sometimes even hostile ones.

In addition, as one would expect, the respected corporation tends to get the ear of key legislators faster and easier than other companies do, Political Action Committees (PACs) notwithstanding.

Of course, because some investors prefer to invest in large, well-known companies, corporate visibility programs are often linked to investor relations programs.

Finally, if "good companies" do indeed make "good products," the connection between product sales and corporate visibility should be clear.

In short, managing corporate impact demands that you pay as much attention to your corporate image as you devote to product marketing. This ongoing process also helps to establish the baseline of public perception about your company that will become your first line of defense when a crisis erupts.

Not everyone subscribes to this theory. Earlier, we spoke of packaged-goods companies, such as Procter & Gamble (P&G), that have worked hard to downplay their corporate image, preferring instead to develop product identities. When a controversy developed around the P&G logo, the company's first reaction was to scarcely acknowledge the problem, believing that most people don't necessarily connect P&G with a particular product. However, once the controversy began to have a negative effect on sales, P&G swallowed its pride and downplayed its century-old symbol to near invisibility. As we have said, corporate visibility has not been a major item on the P&G public relations agenda.

The promotion of the corporate image is an important concern, and corporate visibility programs have become commonplace at most major corporations.

BEING VISIBLE

Now that you have decided that corporate visibility is something you want, how do you get it?

First, there arises a question of what differentiates visibility from mere noise about the company. Many large companies wallpaper the world with an endless stream of press releases on such crucial developments as the promotion of the deputy assistant to the president to the loftier rank of special assistant to the president. Such releases can increase visibility for the company, but mainly among the extended family, neighbors, and fellow alumni of the honoree.

This type of run-of-the-mill publicity does little to enhance the corporate image because it tells little about what the company believes in or supports (an exception would be a personnel release announcing the promotion of a minority employee to a senior position).

Chapter 5

What you need is a way to convince people that your company is more than a loading dock and accounts receivable department—that it contributes to society, whether in terms of technological advancement, cultural or educational support, or just plain leadership in an era when true leaders are rare and then often come with clay feet.

One way to help people see past the corporate veneer and into the "real you" is by displaying one or more of the following attributes:

- evincing intelligence
- taking a stand on an issue
- being generous
- sponsoring a popular event, or if all else fails
- associating with a popular event or cause.

With a little luck, you will display the first attribute—intelligence—all the time, but you can also seek out ways to demonstrate your abilities in a more structured forum. Of course, the most desirable way would be to convince the *Wall Street Journal* or *Business Week* to publish a profile of you in which you are referred to as "XYZ's Resident Genius, Tom Smith," or "Holding degrees from Harvard, Princeton, Yale, and MIT, Smith believes that . . ." Even if you are fortunate enough to have such an article appear, it's unreasonable to expect the *Journal* to run another like it very soon, if ever. Your brain, as such, is only news once (although what comes out of it in the way of new products, theories, or the like is another matter). And for most of us mortals, such articles virtually never come along, especially when we'd most like them to appear.

Let's focus on the other three attributes and hope that intelligence comes along for the ride.

TAKING A STAND

It's not hard to think of CEOs who have gained widespread publicity for their views on a particular issue. J. Peter Grace's pronouncements on the federal budget deficit (and subsequent convening of the Grace Commission) are one example. H. Ross Perot's musings on the state of American (and specifically, Texan) public education are another, and almost everyone in the business seems to know T. Boone Pickens's thoughts about shareholder rights.

These executives didn't become captains of industry just because they had interesting things to say, but now that they have made their mark on American business, people tend to pay attention when they speak. And, as evidenced by the sheer volume of press attention given these men while their personal crusades have been hot, speaking out on issues—especially controversial issues—is a fine way to stay in the public eye.

The issue may have absolutely nothing to do with how affairs are conducted at their companies, but the visibility that a CEO and his or her company get from such a campaign can have a major positive effect on corporate identity.

In 1986, following the annual publication of *Fortune's* "Most Admired Corporations" list, a secondary research project was undertaken, using several computer databases to track the visibility of the top executives of the firms cited as "most admired."

The results were enlightening, if not altogether surprising: The CEOs of America's "Most Admired" companies were quoted in the major business press far more often than the CEOs of less admired companies. A qualitative analysis showed that a significant number of quotations related to issues and took a stand ("We're for it;" "We're against it").

One treads carefully here. BankAmerica executives were widely quoted, too, and that institution made the wrong list (least admired). Still, while a "chicken-or-egg" argument may be made here, even BankAmerica's visibility supports the theory that there is a correlation between the esteem in which a company is held (very high or very low) and the degree to which its executives show up in the press.

Yet, the experience of these high-echelon types is not typical. For the average executive—a regular guy with his initial in the middle, who isn't known to have the U.S. president's ear; who hasn't been able to wangle a seat on the General Motors board; and who can't strike terror in the heart of a CEO by buying 3 percent of a company's stock with a personal check—it is not always so easy to capture the attention of those to whom he or she has something to say.

For one thing, why would anyone listen to what the CEO of a company that makes ironing board covers has to say about the federal deficit when J. Peter Grace has said all there is to say: The deficit is too high; the government spends too much money; and here are 2000 ways to cut back. Got anything to add to that?

To make issues work for you, you have to pick carefully and be prepared to bring a new perspective or dramatically new information to the discussion. Such was the challenge put before one major agency (it happened to be Burson–Marsteller) by Pitney Bowes.

To all the world, Pitney Bowes did one thing and did it well: It made postage meters. The company had developed the product and marketed it so well that the postage-meter market was virtually saturated. The trouble was that Pitney Bowes made other things besides postage meters— copiers and other mail-room equipment—that no one seemed to know about. Media attention was almost nonexistent. Reporters could only seem to associate Pitney Bowes with postage meters, and postage meters stopped being interesting to write about when just about everyone had one. Pitney Bowes was a victim of its own success.

Aside from the unfortunate effect this had on sales, the Wall Street crowd began to feel that the company had gone past its prime. Compounding the problem was the fact that the CEO, Fred T. Allen, was not well known. Analysts simplistically translated a lack of visibility with a lack of business acumen and assumed that the company would not be able to diversify into other product lines—an assumption made ridiculous in retrospect because the company had already done so.

The company needed to find a way to break out of the mold it was being squeezed into, and it was looking for a way to highlight the intelligence and leadership of the CEO. With the agency's help, Pitney Bowes identified "corporate ethics" as a topic in which Allen believed and about which he could speak effectively. Specifically, it was determined that he should focus on the ethical problems faced by companies engaged in international commerce. A speaking engagement scheduled before the Swiss-American Chamber of Commerce in Zurich was selected as the kickoff point for Allen's campaign. Before he could get started, though, the issue had to be broadened so that it would be of interest to as wide an audience as possible. That is, Allen would not make a big hit by going to Zurich, declaring that Pitney Bowes was a paragon of ethical behavior, and decrying the ethically bankrupt behavior of other companies—it would be too obviously self-serving. To make an effective presentation, Allen would have to speak to and for the entire international business community. That tall order required some research.

The agency team commissioned an Opinion Research Corporation survey of Fortune 500 executives on the issue of overseas payoffs, and the results were, to say the least, unexpected. Fifty percent of the executives interviewed believed that bribes should not be paid to foreign officials. That was the good news. The bad news was that the other half of the sample disagreed, saying that paying bribes was just a way of doing business abroad, and that no amount of federal regulation would stop it.

By using the survey results as the basis of his Zurich speech, Allen became a focal point of the growing issue of corporate ethics, which was becoming a "hot" topic in the media in the wake of the McDonnell Douglas bribery scandal. The agency took it from there.

The speech was provided to the *Wall Street Journal* on the

day it was given. It ran on the Op–Ed page the next day, ultimately generating more than 3000 requests for copies of the speech.

Through additional speaking engagements and interviews, Allen was increasingly identified with the issue. This previously unheard-of purveyor of postage meters was revealed to be a dynamic business leader in touch with the important business issues of the day, maybe even a little ahead of the issues.

He appeared in a *Time* cover story, opined in *Newsweek*, and was featured in *Business Week*. Millions of breakfasters saw Allen interviewed by Tom Brokaw on "Today." Before long, he was asked to serve as head of the National Ethics Committee and testified before Congress on the subject of corporate ethics.

Once firmly established as a national figure, Allen continued to speak out on such additional matters as equal opportunity for women and employee relations. As Allen could attest, crime may or may not pay, but talking about it almost certainly does, and you don't even have to talk a lot if you have the right twist.

Those points were graphically made by Burns International Security Services, whose business was preventing crime, not talking about it. Confidentiality was extremely important to Burns and its clients, and for this reason, the firm refused to grant interviews, which it viewed as too uncontrolled. It did, however, agree to provide a speaker for the Executives Club of Chicago, but to talk about what? Like Pitney Bowes, which could have focused on postage meters as an issue and wisely opted not to, Burns could have discussed the finer points of patrolling waste treatment plants. Alas, not too many people would have been interested and, more to the point, such a speech would have perpetuated a misconception about Burns: that it was just a security guard company.

In fact, much of the company's growth was taking place in the corporate world, thanks to an upsurge in white-collar crime. Here was a subject of acute interest to the business community. The text of that one speech was turned into a series of bylined articles in trade publications, and the articles that appeared could themselves be used as sales materials. In a remarkably short time, Burns was able to create a new image for itself and generate several new business leads—all through the presentation and subsequent distribution of one speech before a group of 600 executives.

Not every executive is good at public speaking, but fortunately this tactic can be used very effectively in writing. Op-Ed articles are an excellent way to explore complicated issues in a forum that is accorded a tremendous amount of respect. Many people feel that even if they violently disagree with what you are saying, the fact that you are saying it on the Op-Ed page of the *New York Times* implies a certain credibility.

As we noted, this technique of achieving visibility can have its drawbacks. For example, if your primary target audience is suburban homeowners and you (speaking in your role as CEO) come out strongly in favor of suburban neighborhood shelters for the homeless, you could put your business in jeopardy. Even though the issue may be timely and you stand on the side of the angels, you would be well-advised to consider some other issue for your company to pursue. Of course, you personally can be an advocate for almost anything without putting your business at risk. When the weight of your company, which individuals cannot match, is put behind an issue, your customers grow resentful and act against your company.

What are the issues of the day? On a local level, they can range from the quality of education available to the community to the beautification of the village green. If you are in touch with the concerns of your local community, you will see opportunities to speak out and become an active participant in finding solutions.

National issues can be brought home. There are a number of major concerns facing the United States in general that could be used as a local or regional platform, especially if your principal business is in any way related. Here's a short list of them, along with some types of businesses that have a natural affinity:

- the care of the homeless (clothing, food processing)
- the care of the elderly (pharmaceuticals)
- the deterioration of out-of-print library books (printing, publishing, paper manufacturing)
- affordable, safe child care (any company with a large clerical work force)
- restoration and maintenance of historic homes or buildings (building products, paint, etc.)
- glaucoma (optics)
- education (computers, publishing)

There are many others—use your imagination. Select the

problem, decide what you are prepared to do about it, and design a communications program to support your efforts. And . . . put your money where your mouth is: Back up your good ideas with financial support.

CORPORATE PHILANTHROPY

If your company donates money to charities and causes, you undoubtedly feel pretty good about it, and you should. We have entered what appears to be a long-term period in which the private sector will be called upon to make up the difference between public funding and the real needs of thousands of not-for-profit organizations.

On the other hand, most companies receive far more solicitations for contributions than they can honor, and at some point someone within the organization has to decide which requests will be granted.

In order to make these judgments, some criteria have to be developed. Look at the contributions your company made last year and think about why those organizations were chosen over all the others.

Here is a list of the most commonly given reasons:

1. We gave money to them the year before.
2. The chairman's wife is on the board of the organization.
3. They were the first organization to ask.
4. A valued employee asked us to do so.

5. A big customer asked us to do so.
6. An employee died, and we made a contribution in his name.

Of these typical reasons, the only unassailable one is number six. It is always appropriate to make such contributions, but as they are generally on the order of $100 or so, they should not represent a substantial portion of your contributions budget.

The rest of the all-too-common reasons are at best questionable, though not always unfounded. There are times when you simply have to bite the bullet and buy a table at a banquet to please a major customer or the chairman's wife. Nevertheless, even allowing for such contingencies, most companies lack a clear, sensible policy for corporate contributions, which means that many such grants serve no other purpose than simple philanthropy.

But, should they? What about just giving money away because an organization needs it and it's the right thing to do? We aren't questioning the need or the motivation. We are simply suggesting that because you can't give as much money as you might wish to every organization that asks for it and inevitably you will have to turn some organizations down completely, you should be sure that you select carefully the organizations you will support and that your contributions are substantial enough to be considered very important.

We are in no way suggesting that strategic considerations should be the sole or even major determinant in deciding to whom you will give money, but there is nothing wrong with being guided in your giving strategy by a philosophy of enlightened self-interest. If you do good things, what's wrong with getting credit for them among your key audience groups?

Most CEOs are remarkably shy about the whole matter. They donate money, often large amounts of it, but then seem embarrassed to mention it—they are content with a one-line mention in the ballet troupe's season program. This almost studied reluctance to be recognized for philanthropic support can be traced back to the days of the robber barons. Many of these early, often ruthless, industrial pioneers—remember, these were the tycoons who lived by the words of William Henry Vanderbilt: "The public be damned!"—believed that the Christian ethic mandated that they give away great portions of their fortunes, preferably anonymously, before going off to that great steel mill or railroad in the sky.

Charity at the end of one's life was as much a matter of contrition as of good will—it was the ticket to heaven. To have blown one's horn about it would have negated the virtue behind the gift. The power (and the wealth) of these remarkable men can be seen in the monuments bearing their names that they left behind, but many more millions of dollars went (unheralded) to charities all over the country.

Today, the money behind corporate contributions usually does not come from personal fortunes—it is siphoned off, pre-tax, from corporate profits—profits that might otherwise go to shareholders. If we agree that corporate philanthropy is a good thing, we must also recognize that shareholders have a right to know that you are getting as much from your largesse as you are from cost-cutting strategies in your manufacturing process. It's their money you're giving away (although we will not go as far as the fractious economist Milton Friedman, who suggests that virtually any corporate largesse directed at anyone but the shareholders is corporate irresponsibility). We believe that corporate contributions are important and that they are certainly a vital part of managing corporate impact.

Even if your company is not publicly traded, why give money to an organization simply because it is the first one to ask you for it? There may be 10 other organizations with equally worthy missions, equal need, and, notably, a logical connection to the business you are in or to your key audiences.

The first step is to identify the types of organizations or causes that it makes sense for your company to support. We note that two fairly sacred cows—the matching of employee contributions to United Way and matching gifts to colleges and secondary schools—may eat up a significant chunk of your contributions budget, despite the fact that the recognition factor for the company in either of these two programs is next to nil. Still, United Way gives your employees the feeling that they are helping less fortunate others, especially when their own contributions are extended by a company match. Matching employee gifts to educational institutions—the ultimate in "old school tie" behavior—will continue for as long as there are old schools.

These exceptions noted, there comes the question of how to divide up whatever funds are left in the contributions budget, and a logical, orderly process is called for.

First, consider how much money you have to give away. If it is a fairly modest sum, say $20,000 to $50,000, it may make sense to limit your philanthropy to one or two substantial gifts, rather than to split up the money into 50 or more small gifts.

If your objective is to favorably impress upscale consumers, a gift to the local ballet makes sense. Remember, however, that major corporations and the National Endowment for the Arts may be making far bigger gifts than you can afford, and you may get lost in the shuffle. You can avoid being overshadowed by larger donors by working with the organization's staff to identify a particular project or need that your company can "own"—say, the design and printing costs of the annual calendar—with the proviso that your company be prominently identified as the major benefactor. Otherwise, your $10,000 gift may simply be recognized as one of many listings in the "$10,000-and-above" category—which is only slightly better than "anonymous."

The next consideration should be the theme or direction of your philanthropy. For example, you may feel strongly that the company's philanthropy should be used to support improvements in education. If so, you have legitimately and simply ruled out contributions to any organizations that are concerned with something else. Over time, that commitment becomes known, and you will experience a sharp reduction in requests from other types of organizations—another benefit of narrowing your sights.

Suppose your company, let's say it's in Syracuse, New York, wants to support some aspect of the arts and has about $50,000 to spend over and above United Way contributions and matching grants to employee alma maters. How should the money be divided up?

Maybe it shouldn't be divided at all. If you split up the $50,000 into fifty $1000 gifts, your total impact is going to be considerably less than if you choose wisely and give the whole sum to one organization.

Apply strict criteria to each request for a donation. Is it in line with your stated interests? Is the cause or organization something your target audiences care about? Will they be impressed to see your name listed among the contributors? Will they ever see your name? Can your contribution make a substantial impact? Well, if you make a contribution to the Syracuse Stage, it's likely to have a greater impact for you than a similar contribution to the Metropolitan Opera. You don't have enough money to garner the same attention Texaco receives for its millions, and your Syracuse customer base doesn't get down to the city too often.

Another factor is how the money will be used—don't forget that you do have a say in how the money is spent. Will the money be used for operating expenses? Bricks and mortar? Endowment? Operating expenses is the least desirable disposition of a contribution—no one ever seems to remember whose money kept the lobby lights burning. A new wing with your company's name on it is far superior. Endowment falls somewhere in the middle.

Then, and this is important (although it's the part many executives seem to have the most trouble with): What's in it for you? How will the recipient of your contribution acknowledge it publicly? With a line buried in the season program? With an opening-night reception? Will they handle the publicity? Even if the answer to this last one is yes, you should figure on supporting any such efforts yourself. Generating publicity around your contribution (tasteful, of course, not breast-beating, self-congratulatory puffery) is the whole point of making a "strategic contribution." Otherwise, it's not strategic at all; it's charity, and your shareholders may not be terribly supportive of your generosity.

SPONSORING POPULAR EVENTS

As we have noted, sponsoring special events is a popular way for companies to increase their visibility. Some of the events companies sponsor year after year are household names nationwide, even though the events themselves are regional: Manufacturers Hanover and the New York City Marathon; Macy's and the Thanksgiving Day Parade; and the JVC Jazz Festival are but three such spectaculars occurring each year in New York that receive national media attention.

These events are noteworthy because they are single-sponsor events. That means that whenever the media refer to the event, they tend to include the sponsor's name. Joint sponsorship, such as is typical for the U.S. Open Tennis Championship in New York, tends to result in little or no direct press attention, although the sponsor's banners are omnipresent (as are their television commercials). However, sponsors of the U.S. Open, for example, do get hospitality areas for entertaining prized clients and bigwig visitors, large quantities of September's hottest tickets, and opportunities to rub elbows with the world's top tennis pros. Those perks may be enough for some companies.

Joint sponsorship also suggests that the sponsors have not actually organized anything—just paid a lot of money to be associated with the event. That can be the case in sole-sponsor events, too, but very often, particularly with regional events, the sponsor not only funds the event, but provides people to help run it, and may even manage the entire event. On the local level, golf tournaments and semi-pro sports teams are typical sponsorship opportunities.

Sponsorship differs from charitable support by virtue of the fact that nearly everyone involved in a sponsorship is trying to make a profit—including (usually, if not especially) the group or person requesting the support. Sponsoring a Little League team would be an exception.

Sponsorship works because people who feel good about the event will likely feel good about the company that made it all possible, and (dare we repeat) "good companies" make "good products."

The trick is to sponsor something that means something to your target audience. Obviously, if you're trying to appeal to upmarket consumers, sponsorship of Bowling For Dollars isn't for you.

One of our favorite examples of perfect targeting was provided by The Equitable Life Assurance Society of the United States. The Equitable was looking for an event that would appeal to relatively affluent folks all over the country; emphasize family values; promote physical fitness; and end with a nationally visible climax. What they came up with was The Equitable Family Tennis Challenge, now in its fourteenth year.

The idea was simple enough: The demographic profile for the "average" tennis player (mean income: $50,000 in 1984) was ideal for this diversified financial services company, and The Equitable's far-flung agent network made local tie-ins practical.

The tournament, which pairs family members—mother/daughter, father/son, husband/wife, brother/sister, father/daughter and mother/son—encourages families to play together and promotes physical fitness.

The Challenge begins each year with local matches held at neighborhood courts. From there, winners advance to the sectional tournaments, with sectional winners and their families receiving an all-expenses-paid trip to New York to compete in the finals at the National Tennis Center during the U.S. Open.

In 1986, more than 87,000 pairs competed in the Tennis Challenge, making it the largest amateur sporting event in the world. For a surprisingly affordable cost, The Equitable benefited well, especially considering the extraordinary visibility given to the Challenge by both the local media, who track the progress of local players as they advance through the different rounds of competition, and the national media, as the finalists receive their trophies in a live, televised ceremony at Center Court during a break between two U.S. Open final matches.

Admittedly, The Equitable is a national organization with a substantial budget for such things. But you can emulate its success on a regional level. You can underwrite a local amateur sports team, for instance. Establish the XYZ Sportsmanship Award for the high school athlete of the week. Underwrite the cost of having a local choral group sing holiday carols in the business district. Pay the honorarium to invite a regional or even national celebrity to come and speak to a local group or at a school. Host a reception in conjunction with the arrival of a traveling art exhibition or orchestra performance. (In many cases, the immediate beneficiary of your largesse—say, the music hall that will sell more tickets thanks to your reception—will help you coordinate these activities and can help generate publicity for them.)

Whatever you select, figure that you will spend at least half again the actual cost of the event for publicity and advertising to make sure you turn out a crowd—and to make sure everyone knows whose generosity made the event possible.

PUTTING ALL THREE TOGETHER

One way to combine all three tactics—taking a stand, charitable support, and sponsorship—is to underwrite the activities of a leading proponent of a given issue. It is a very passive way to be involved, but it fills two typical needs of such organizations: financial support and the credibility of corporate acceptance.

One of the more well-known examples is the "Just Say No" anti-drug abuse campaign, which has garnered considerable corporate support. Another popular cause is the search for missing children. Dairies have been very active on a local level in this effort; many have printed the photographs of missing children on their milk cartons. Under the "Only in New York" category, metropolitan-area Burger King restaurants donated funds to buy bullet-proof vests for police officers during the city's past fiscal crisis.

Other examples are slightly less altruistic—such as when a company offers to donate a percentage of its profits to a non-profit organization (Muscular Dystrophy Association, United States Olympic Committee, etc.) for each hamburger, paperback book, ice cream sundae, or ball-point pen sold. We say it is less altruistic because, obviously, the company is benefiting from the public's participation at least as much as the charity is.

6

Hammers and Nails

Tools for Generating Publicity

The three areas we focused on for generating corporate visibility—issues, charity, and events—are strategies. To bring your strategies to life, you need some specialized tools.

Although we did not set out to write a "how-to" book on basic publicity techniques, we do want to spend a little time reviewing some of the tactics, or tools, you can use to bring attention to yourself—in a manner that doesn't do more harm than good.

Not every tool is useful in every situation, but it's good to have a choice. As Jim Dowling, Burson-Marsteller CEO, puts it: "If your only tool is a hammer, the answer to every problem is a nail." Not every product introduction calls for a press conference; not every well-heeled consumer wants to go to a free seminar on tax strategies for the affluent.

Here, then, in a logical sequence are the most common tools you will use to generate visibility.

THE PRESS RELEASE

The workhorse of public relations, the press release, can be an effective means of disseminating information about your company. It can also be a great waste of time and money, if not done properly.

There are dozens of ways to write a "successful" press release, and by successful, we mean one that is used for its intended purpose by the person receiving it.

Press releases are also often called "News Releases," which is an apt description since the purpose of the releases is to convey news. Often they do not, or the news is of such limited interest that it does not find its way into the media. Obviously, the greater the number of people likely to be interested in your announcement, the greater its chances of being covered. Given a limited amount of space for management change stories, a *New York Times* editor will have more interest in the announcement of a new CEO at a major bank than a new CEO at a Wayne, New Jersey, real estate agency. The editor of the local paper in Wayne would probably feel quite the opposite.

Be realistic in your expectations and select your media accordingly. *Times* editors—all editors, for that matter— routinely complain that they're buried daily under piles of press releases they can't use. This practice makes them irritable and inclined to throw away, unopened, envelopes with certain logos adorning them.

Help the editor provide a service to his or her readers. Put your release into an easily digested format. Automatically delete the following words wherever they may be found:

- astounding
- tremendous
- extraordinary (unless accompanied by "gain")
- phenomenal
- incredible
- awesome
- remarkable
- miraculous

(Incredibly, this astounding list actually has been drawn from awesome press releases we have received from phenomenal client wordsmiths.)

Be sure to include a dateline or have the date of release clearly in evidence somewhere. Also be sure to list prominently the name and telephone number of a person who can be contacted by the editor for clarification or more information.

Strive to use headlines that really convey the subject of a release—they can be catchy, but avoid being too cute, especially if the subject matter is relatively dry, like a promotion announcement. "XYZ Appoints Smith Executive Vice President" is more effective than, say, "Onward and Upward: Smith Takes a Giant Step."

Observe the old journalistic notion of the inverted pyramid: Put your biggest news at the top of the release and list facts of decreasing importance in succeeding paragraphs. If a release must run to more than one page, imagine that page two might be lost in a mailroom shuffle. Does page one get the main point across, and does it have your name and number on it as discussed?

Once you have sent or delivered your press release, follow up. Call the reporter or editor to whom you sent a release and confirm that it arrived safely. Ask if the editor has any additional questions. (This technique may help to ensure that the release is actually read.)

Press releases need not even be sent to the press to be effective. We once had a client who needed to reach a fairly small group of customers with some news; there was some concern that these customers wouldn't see the item in the trade journals to which the release had been sent. The particular news item—that the client had upgraded its computerized order-processing system—wasn't significant enough to warrant a personal letter, but the client wanted to remind customers that the company was always getting better. Why not, we suggested, just send the customer the release, with a little note from the client saying: "Just thought you might like to see this . . . ."

So successful was the response—several customers actually took the time to drop a few lines to our client thanking him for his trouble—that for successive news releases, the mailing list included more customers than publications. Sending the release in an almost offhand manner was an easy and inexpensive way to maintain a level of contact with the customer, while saving the personal letter or visit for something really important.

Remember, too, that just because the news item in a press release isn't deemed important enough by a publication to warrant a mention on its own doesn't mean it's not worth sending. Editors of trade publications in particular will want to know everything that's going on in the industry they serve and will keep the release on file. Maybe an upgraded computer system isn't big news now, but it may well be that a feature article on computerization in the industry is slated to appear a few months down the road, and then that press release may be very handy.

At the same time, the significance of the new computer system is relative—a *Business Week* editor isn't likely to care much about the upgraded system and will consider the release to be one more piece of junk mail cluttering the desk. Don't waste the postage—or the editor's time.

THE PRESS CONFERENCE

In its most basic form, the press conference is simply a gathering of reporters in one place to hear what you have to say. Members of Congress hold them on the Capitol steps. Mayor Koch of New York City has been known to have them almost anywhere, including the panda enclosure at the Bronx Zoo. But most companies prefer to hold them at their premises or in a hotel or other controllable environment.

In general, press conferences are a highly overrated and overused means of communicating with the media. Press conferences should be reserved for really special occasions. When you have something particularly noteworthy to announce, a press conference can be an efficient means of reaching all relevant media simultaneously. However, if the news you have to convey is less than momentous, stop and consider whether you can accomplish the same basic dissemination of news by means of hand-delivered press kits and one-on-one telephone interviews as requested (more on this subject in the section on Media Alerts).

Some press conferences include a luncheon or full breakfast. Some (for certain consumer products) can get quite elaborate. In an extremely creative event staged to introduce their Betamovie videocamera, Sony Corporation's agency converted the Tavern On The Green restaurant in

New York City into a circus, with clowns, jugglers, and performing animals. Reporters were invited to bring their children, and, using proffered videocameras, to tape their children enjoying the fun. The cost of the event to Sony was breathtaking, but press coverage was excellent, and Sony considered the money well spent.

Public relations professionals have their own personal horror stories about press conferences. Most of these stories have to do with the failure of the press to attend, due to some cataclysmic event. One which comes to mind is the press conference called by a company at 2:00 p.m., March 30, 1981 at a hotel in Washington, D.C. The public relations agency coordinating the press conference had worked hard to assure a good turnout of the press, including camera crews from several of the local television stations.

As the news crews were traveling to the hotel, Ronald Reagan was walking out of another hotel across town—the Washington Hilton—where he had his fateful encounter with John Hinckley and a .22 caliber slug. Coverage of the client's press conference was disappointing.

(On the other hand, when a winter's worst blizzard threatened to keep reporters at their desks instead of attending a General Foods press conference, the situation was salvaged by some quick thinking on the agency's part: Limousines were dispatched to transport reporters to and from the press conference in unaccustomed splendor—unaccustomed even in sunny weather!)

Yet notwithstanding such unforeseen calamities, a typical press conference will unfold as planned. However, it must be planned with almost military precision—a good deal of thought should go into anticipating what could go wrong.

We once organized a press conference to introduce a new software product. We had at first recommended simply putting the new software into the hands of the most important software reviewers and doing one-on-one interviews, but the software had such broad applications that a press conference seemed worth doing.

Every detail was scrutinized. Our strategy was to have the president of the company make a few brief remarks, which we had scripted, and then let the product do the talking. Product demonstrations would be given in various corners of the room. These were the key, because part of the software's appeal was its fancy graphics (which couldn't be captured in a photograph) and the speed with which it did whatever it did. (It was a database management product.)

The software was new and different enough that over 75 reporters accepted invitations to attend the press conference. Of course, the fact that it was held in a private room at The Four Seasons and included lunch may have enticed some to attend. In any case, we were delighted with the turnout.

At the appointed time, the VP of marketing summoned the attention of the throng and introduced the company president with a flourish. The president strode to the podium and said, "Our PR agency wrote these remarks, but I don't think they convey the true significance of this product. Let me take you back to how it all began. . . ."

After the first five minutes, it became clear that he wasn't going to respond to subtle gestures from the back of the room (drawing one's finger across one's throat, for example, or tapping one's watch), and our lives flashed before our eyes. For the next 45 minutes, he droned on about the company he had founded; how gratifying it was to have the press here after years of being ignored; and how no one wants to give the little guy a chance. . . . He went on and on. And on.

By the time he had finished, several reporters looked glassy eyed, a few had left, and those who hadn't alternated between unsubtle yawns and career-withering glances at us. Most of the reporters who remained only did so long enough to collect their press kits—they now had no time to hang around for the demonstrations.

Press coverage was minimal, expenses were high, and to salvage the product introduction, we ended up doing what we had suggested in the first place: providing copies of the software to the major computer publications and working with writers individually. Coverage from that tactic was better, but the press conference was already tepid water under the bridge.

THE MEDIA ALERT

The Media Alert, or Request for Coverage, is simply a way to notify print and broadcast media that something interesting is going to happen and invite them to witness it. It clearly indicates where and when the event (a press conference, photo opportunity, ribbon-cutting ceremony) will take place and the basic significance of the event. For daily papers and electronic media, such alerts are usually sent out fairly close to the date of the actual event. Follow up on these with telephone calls, both to confirm receipt and to get a sense of the recipients' interest in attending.

One of the fallacies often heard about media alerts is that it is suicide to actually tell reporters what is going to happen at the event—lest they decide it's not worth covering. Remember that television news depends on a video presentation. If, on hearing what the event is about, the station declines to send a film crew out, it's because the story just isn't going to yield good pictures. A press conference in which the company president announces a joint venture with a competitor may have some news value, but it's not very interesting to watch.

On the other hand, print reporters are a naturally wary lot. When they are invited to a "media event," they want to know what it will be about. Use this skepticism to test whether you really need to have a press conference at all: If telling the reporter the most basic fact of what's going to happen—the announcement of a joint venture between ABC Company and XYZ Company—would give so much away that the reporter wouldn't need to come, you'd be better off just announcing the news via a press release and offering company spokespersons for telephone interviews. Reporters don't have the time to traipse all over town chasing stories about small companies doing (relatively) small deals. However, if the joint venture is between, say, an IBM and an AT&T, that would be news—but how much of a story could reporters write if that was all they knew? Tell them the time and place—they'll be there.

By attempting to keep essentially unexciting news—unexciting to the vast majority of a publication's readers—shrouded in mystery until the climactic announcement, you are making a reporter's already hectic life more difficult. That's no way to foster good relations with the press.

The media alert can also be a stand-alone publicity tactic. In 1981, the "All-Saver Certificate," the immediate forerunner of the Individual Retirement Account (IRA), was being introduced with great fanfare. All major banks offered them, so the challenge was to find a way to stand out from the crowd. Citibank sent out a media alert announcing that its branches would remain open until midnight on the last day that certificates would be offered at a particularly high interest rate (the rate was tied to fluctuations in certain government securities, and the certificate locked up a depositor's money for an extended period).

The alert noted which branches were convenient to the broadcast studios of local newscasts and indicated that a spokesperson would be available for commentary.

With no other mailings or calls to support it, the media alert did its job: Over 90 percent of the coverage of the mad rush to get the All-Saver Certificate at the favorable rate focused on Citibank—despite the fact that the same rate was available at all major banks and several others also stayed open late.

Chapter 6

THE PRESS KIT

Sometimes used as take-alongs from press conferences, press kits are also often mailed to reporters for background purposes. Essentially, the press kit is a folder into which are placed press releases describing new products, services, key personnel, and the company itself, along with black and white photos. If practical, product samples or a token reminder or replica can be enclosed as well.

THE OP-ED ARTICLE

An Op-Ed article, named for its usual position on the "Op-Ed page" (the page opposite the editorial page in a newspaper), is a bylined article that generally deals with political, social, or economic issues of the day. It is most often employed to try to change broad public opinion, usually calling for some action—eliminating unfair subsidies or ending the arms race, for example.

Obviously, an Op-Ed in the *New York Times* or the *Washington Post* is one of the best means of reaching large numbers of influential people, and, as a result, placing an Op-Ed in these newspapers is a difficult assignment. A local paper, while particularly interested in Op-Ed articles pertaining to local problems, can still be an effective forum for discussing national issues, particularly when the objective is to develop a ground swell of popular support. In such a case, an Op-Ed campaign can be especially useful.

If you are trying to generate support around the country for a particular point of view—say, the unconstitutionality of a proposed piece of legislation—a sample Op-Ed article can be written that supports your contention. Then, a dozen or so experts from different states, who share your opinion, can be asked to take the Op-Ed as their own. Invite them to personalize it and make it relevant to their local communities. You may then offer to handle the placement of the article in the most influential newspaper in their area, although the expert will often have better contacts at that paper than you do. This tactic is a win–win project. You have elicited a respectable third-party endorsement while giving the expert a chance to enhance his or her own reputation.

THE BYLINED ARTICLE

Similar in concept to the Op-Ed article, the bylined article is a useful tool for demonstrating the specific expertise and approach of a key individual to either a business or consumer audience. Topics have no bounds—your thoughts on trends in the property insurance business or ten tips on cutting costs in data processing, for instance. Your area of expertise, whatever it is, is fodder for such an article.

As for the writing, you can do it, or you can have the article ghostwritten by a staff person or your public relations agency. Generally speaking, a 1000- to 1200-word article is sufficient, although an editor may have his or her own particular requirements. When you submit the article, double-spaced with wide margins, offer to make revisions if the piece does not precisely fit the editor's requirements. Even so, expect the editor to edit the article to make it conform to space restrictions or the style of the magazine. Naturally, you may take a lot of pride in your authorship, but resist the temptation to complain if an article is published in a slightly different form than when you submitted it—so long as it reflects well on your knowledge, it has served its purpose.

Once the article is in print, inquire about the magazine's reprint policy. Many publications offer a high-quality reprint service at a reasonable price. If not, ask about securing permission to reprint the article, giving credit to the publication. These reprints can be used as mailers to your existing and prospective clients or customers. Do not simply photocopy the article and send it along—it is a blatant violation of the U.S. copyright laws.

THE EDITORIAL BOARD MEETING

If you are involved in a really big issue, such as free trade or tax reform, it may be possible to meet with the editorial board of a major newspaper. The purpose is twofold. First, with some luck and a convincing story, you may impel the editors to write an editorial in support of your cause. Second, if the editors come to understand your side of an issue, the tone of the paper's coverage may change, in the way a story is written or edited. All newspapers are written from a point of view, in spite of sincere efforts to remain objective. You can influence that point of view—you can even turn it around 180 degrees.

THE PITCH LETTER

Most press relations activities begin with a pitch letter. It is the basic sales tool of media relations. Most reporters and editors dislike receiving suggestions by telephone, and with good reason. Because they work under tight deadlines, they can't afford to be tied up with long telephone conversations in the middle of the day. Instead, they prefer to receive story ideas in letter form, which are then read at a more convenient time and routed to the appropriate editorial department.

Some of the most creative writing in a public relations program goes into pitch letters. But, for a basic publicity effort, if you have selected your media properly, a pitch letter needs "just the facts": the who, what, when, where, and why. What you're trying to accomplish is to interest the reporter or editor in covering your company, either by attending an event or by interviewing a spokesperson. You should also include a brief pitch letter with bylined articles you have written but have not preplaced. In this case, the letter should provide a synopsis of the article so that the editor does not have to read the whole piece to know if it is of potential interest to his or her readers. A really well done letter can get an otherwise ignored article read.

THE ONE-ON-ONE INTERVIEW

The one-on-one (or "exclusive") interview is just what it sounds like it is: You or your spokesperson meet with a reporter, who (with luck) writes a favorable article. In a sense, a press conference would be the opposite of the one-on-one interview.

The interview provides the reporter with an opportunity

to look beyond the products and financial statements a company produces, to get a feeling for the man or woman at the top. It's a chance to become acquainted with a CEO or other senior executive and learn how he or she feels about specific developments at the company or within the industry.

On the other hand, the person being interviewed should look at the one-on-one as a chance to show off why the company has become so successful (or someday will be) and why he or she is the right person to be at the helm.

Never go into any interview unprepared. Before you agree to an interview, ask what the reporter wants to talk about and do your homework. If the last quarter's results were not as good as expected, be prepared to summarize why, and outline why you expect an imminent improvement.

Ask yourself, "What are the three things I want that reporter to leave here understanding?" Practice making those points in different ways. You can even write them down on a three-by-five card and keep it handy during the interview—just to remind yourself to keep going back to them.

If the reporter asks a question to which you do not immediately have an answer, offer to get back with the answer after the interview concludes. And be sure you follow through with the offer!

Be honest and open. That doesn't mean you have to give away the store, but remember that any statistics you use to illustrate a point can usually be verified by a reporter through another source and any substantial inaccuracies will be noted.

One more thing: There is no such thing as "off the record." Any comment you make in this fashion tempts the reporter to find and quote someone else saying the same thing or to otherwise verify the information through a third party. Your "off-the-record" comment can then become tomorrow's headline.

THE SEMINAR

The seminar, like the speech, is one of the ways you can demonstrate your expertise to the consumer directly, without channeling your messages through the media. Unlike a speech, which is by definition a passive exercise for the audience, the seminar is often a means of drawing the audience into the goings-on.

Seminars can be on almost any subject, for virtually any type of audience. Industry seminars tend to be rather technical—"Recent Developments in Fire Resistant Polymers," for example. A less technical example would be if a financial institution sponsored a seminar for its affluent customers on tax strategies ('twould be no accident that the sponsor's financial instruments are cited as "sound investment choices").

Luncheon seminars are popular (though not to be confused with client/prospect luncheons, discussed later). Many harried executives can be enticed to attend your program if it includes a meal, allowing them to kill two birds with one stone.

SPEAKING PLATFORMS

Giving speeches before target audiences is another effective means of convincing people that there is a bright light shining behind those baby blues. Platforms range from the local garden club or Rotary to top-of-the-line platforms, such as the Detroit Economic Club. Getting a slot on the program can take a long time, but if you are prepared to move quickly, you can often do yourself a lot of good by agreeing to "fill-in" at the last minute when cancellations occur.

Professional speakers, or high-profile people who just give a lot of speeches, often develop one speech and give it a dozen times in a season, without bothering to personalize it to fit the audience. That's okay for some speakers, such as Tom Peters talking about the passionate search for excellence—presumably that's what he was hired to speak about.

A more effective technique for your purposes is to research the audience and tailor your remarks to be of particular significance to your listeners. It's not so tough, actually, and it shows that you care enough to do something special. Since your goal is to highlight your intelligence and grasp of a subject as a means of developing new business opportunities, it makes sense to begin selling right on the podium.

The organization that has invited you to speak may arrange for press coverage—if not, ask them if they would mind if you invited a local reporter to sit in and listen. Even if they decline (many do), send a copy of the text to the local papers—unless, in high dramatic style, you were so moved by the occasion that you "set your prepared remarks aside" and spoke "from the heart." It would be awkward for the newspaper to report that you spoke to the local Rotary about tax reform when in fact you spoke impassionedly about the evils of program trading on Wall Street.

CLIENT/CUSTOMER LUNCHEONS/DINNERS

These are more social occasions than selling opportunities unto themselves. Arrange for a "name" speaker (a celebrity such as a major business figure, a politician, or a performing artist) to speak on a topical or simply entertaining subject and invite favored clients or prospects for lunch or dinner in a private room. As you become better known in your field, you might eventually be asked to be such a speaker—sometimes in return for having provided a forum for another executive.

These are stroking sessions, and it would be déclassé to try to make a sales pitch over the shrimp bisque. However, it's a time-honored way to keep prized clients happy and impress prospects.

POLITICAL ACTION COMMITTEES (PACS)

PAC contributions, funded by employees who see their employer's political agenda as important to their own future, can be an effective means of getting a legislator's attention, but there is some potential for a backlash in light of current concerns about politicians pandering to special interests. That said, most corporations today have a PAC. In the world of Washington politics (and to a growing degree on the state level, too), it is getting very difficult to arrange even a short meeting with a legislator to whom one has not made a political contribution. These contributions have become practically a cost of doing business. On the other hand, a PAC contribution will only get you the first 10 minutes of a meeting with a legislator—after that, you're on your own.

If your company doesn't have a PAC, consider retaining a lobbying or public relations firm that does.

NEWSLETTERS

These can range from informal, internal roundups of company news—including anniversaries and promotions—to broad-gauged analyses of current events affecting the company's business that are designed for use both internally and externally. At their best, they motivate, instruct, and provoke thought. At their worst, they confuse, trivialize, and eventually, die. It is wise to periodically check with the readership to see if your publication is achieving the communications objectives you have set for it.

SURVEYS

Surveys allow you to contribute to the development of your industry by identifying opinions, attitudes, and trends and reporting them to others who can use such information in their strategic plans. Of course, you, too, will gain useful information, but from a public relations perspective, a survey is a way to underscore your position as a leader of your field. Since the validity of a survey is determined by its methodology and sample, companies often retain professional survey firms to conduct the research. Even so, if you commissioned the survey, it's yours to publicize (with credit to the surveyor).

The most newsworthy surveys are the ones that produce easily understood signs of a shift in how people think or act. One of the most effective techniques you can use is to develop statistical information that allows a reporter to "bring home" a national issue.

For example, every month, the government publishes its statistics on housing starts. What does that number mean? To most people, not much. But if you are a mortgage lender and your mortgage originations were up 10 percent in a given period, that's news. Consider asking construction loan applicants a few questions, such as "Why did you decide to build now?" The answers will form an interesting story for a local reporter, and you'll be quoted as the expert.

7

Grass Roots

What'll the Neighbors Think

DEDMETE INDUSTRIES: A CASE STUDY

The poet Robert Browning's words run through Sam Jones's mind as he pulls into the plant parking lot on this glorious day:

> The year's at the spring
> And day's at the morn . . .
> All's right with the world.

He noses his Mercedes into the parking space with the "Reserved for Mr. Jones" sign. The sun is shining brightly, and the trees lining the perimeter of the plant site are starting to bloom. He's looking dapper in his crisply pressed suit and glistening Italian shoes. As he walks from the car to the office, two factory workers, longtime employees, wave and call hello. He's proud of the fact that he has never lost touch with the "guys on the line," never forgotten that when he was in college, he earned tuition money working in this very plant. And now, the American Dream has come true: He's the president of Dedmete Industries.

"What a beautiful day!" he thinks. He makes a mental note to see if his biggest client, Smith, can leave the office early today. The two of them can get in the back nine at the club, and he can squeeze Smith some more on that megabucks contract.

Birds are chirping cheerily as he takes by twos the steps to the front door of the new executive office complex.

He smiles at the receptionist and compliments her on her

outfit. She smiles back. "It's going to be a great day," he says to himself as he breezes into his handsomely paneled office, thoughts of his new putter filling his head.

His secretary, Ms. Debote, looking strangely harried, follows him in. She hands him a wad of "While-You-Were-Outs," and announces that he has two visitors waiting—Mr. Skull and his assistant, Ms. Crossbones, from the Environmental Protection Agency. Visions of his putter dissolve immediately.

Quickly scanning the messages, he sees they are from:

- the shop steward,
- the fractious head of the local consumer activist group,
- a reporter from the six o'clock news,
- the mayor's office,
- the Right Reverend Hy N. Mighty, representing something called the "Ecumenical Council Against Corporate Irresponsibility,"
- his wife, and
- someone from the Bureau of Indian Affairs.

A thought flashes through his mind—maybe he'd better not call Smith just yet; this could be a tough day.

Ms. Debote ushers in Skull and Crossbones. It's only 9:05 in the morning, and the nightmare has just begun.

Skull reminds him that EPA inspectors have been to the plant site on four separate occasions, taking water and soil samples. As noted in their letter of April 16 ("Letter?" he thinks), the laboratory analysis shows that the company probably has been dumping hazardous chemicals into the environment. The town water supply is in imminent danger of contamination, and the EPA has issued an emergency warning to residents that they should begin drinking bottled water until further notice.

Skull says that in light of the overwhelming evidence against Jones's company, the most expeditious solution would be to sign a consent decree (Crossbones withdraws a two-inch stack of legal documents from her briefcase) and begin to make arrangements to reimburse the Superfund for the approximately $3.7 million cost of cleaning up the site.

Not wanting to make any hasty decisions, Jones asks for a few days to look over the consent decree. Skull agrees, but says that he expects to hear from him within 72 hours. As he gets up to leave, Skull drops the final bombshell. All plant operations will have to be suspended indefinitely during the cleanup. Exit Skull, Crossbones in tow.

Although nearly in shock, Jones has enough presence of mind to tell Ms. Debote to hold his calls and get him the legal department.

The attorneys offer little comfort. They warned him about the April 16 letter when it arrived. (One smug-looking lawyer produces a copy of the interoffice memo. Jones vaguely remembers having seen it, but that was right when he was in the midst of preparing a major sales presentation for Smith Pharmaceuticals, and he couldn't really bother with it then. Before long he had forgotten about the memo and the letter.)

Jones gives the attorneys the consent decree and tells them to get back to him within 48 hours. Exit attorneys.

He turns to the phone messages. First he has Ms. Debote schedule an appointment with the shop steward. She does and reports back that the steward is very agitated, demanding that Jones be prepared to prove that employees are not being placed at grave personal risk by continuing to work at the plant. Jones knows a job action when he smells one. A small throb develops over his eyes.

The consumer activist cannot be reached—at this moment she is staging a press conference at the plant gate. He leaps to the window: sure enough. He acts instinctively, telling Ms. Debote to instruct the guards to keep an eye on the press because he doesn't want pictures of the plant on the front page.

The Mayor's assistant is next. She called about next week's testimonial dinner at which Jones was to be honored for his longtime support of Junior Achievement. The dinner has been canceled because the Mayor will not be feeling well that night.

The Right Reverend Hy N. Mighty is at the press conference, too. When Jones tries to reach him, a local college student who volunteers as the Reverend's assistant answers the phone. The student spends 10 minutes telling Jones about his mother's recent and mysterious death from cancer, how no one else in his family has ever had cancer, how his mother was on a special weight-reduction plan in which she only consumed macadamia nuts and four gallons of water per day, how he's heard about Jones dumping chemicals in the water, and how Jones will be hearing from his lawyer.

Jones's wife is hysterical. A TV news crew tried to film her taking their son to school. The two of them are now prisoners in their house. On an extension phone, his son asks if it's true that he is killing innocent fish and animals. His wife says she's taking the boy to her mother's house for a few days. Jones's head is really banging now.

Mr. Twelve Wolves Howling from the Bureau of Indian Affairs had called to say that he had not received a reply to his letter of February 21, in which he documented that the plant site lies atop an ancient Mohawk burial ground. In light of today's revelation of wanton contamination of the site, he has no alternative but to begin legal proceedings on behalf of the entire Iroquois nation. His staff is sending out a press release this afternoon.

Ms. Debote buzzes. A security guard has just punched out a newspaper photographer covering the press conference. The news crew has gone to live coverage. Jones switches on the television in the corner. The television reporter's voice narrates as Jones watches the action at the gate from his window.

"If you're just tuning in, we're reporting live from Dedmete Industries, where an allegedly crazed security guard has just allegedly assaulted a member of the press who was doing nothing more than taking a harmless photograph of the Dedmete plant. The plant has been identified by the

EPA as the source of the deadly contaminates found in the city's water supply. We tried to reach Mr. Jones, the president of Dedmete, this morning, but not surprisingly, he has not returned our calls. . . . What you're seeing now is the ambulance and paramedics arriving on the scene of this violent confrontation. . . . The police are here and have ordered the angry crowd to disperse. . . ."

Jones's company is Dedmete, and so is Jones.

It's easy enough to say, "Don't let this happen to you!" As a practical matter, though, events such as those that have befallen our friend Jones do happen, and when they do, the time for preventive measures is obviously long past. Remedial measures are what's called for (and there are some options available, even in this mess).

But just as important as reacting well in a crisis is managing one's corporate impact over the previous years—had Jones done so, he might well have been able to nip his problems in the bud. Since he did not, he has some heavy-duty firefighting ahead of him, and he can count on quite a few sleepless nights—maybe months of them.

Jones actually has several different crises on his hands simultaneously. The obvious one is the environmental problem cited by the EPA and the related publicity generated by its disclosure. At the same time, he may be facing a strike by his employees. Even if he escapes that misery, the EPA is threatening to shut down the plant during the cleanup. That means layoffs, and no production means no income, which probably means no debt service and no accounts payable. Ultimately, filing for Chapter 11 protection might be necessary.

Jones has another problem—if he signs the consent decree, in which he admits no guilt but agrees to compensate the EPA for the cost of the cleanup, he may still be opening himself up to a staggering civil liability. The survivors of the late mother with the peculiar diet could probably make a very compelling case before a jury, and the consent decree would only add support to their claims. That family could have lots of company, too; this case might turn out to be perfect for a class action. Finally, there is the matter of liability arising from the guard's alleged assault on the photographer. Both criminal and civil action could result from that incident.

The chances of emerging from this nightmare intact are hopelessly slim. One way or another, Dedmete Industries will be inevitably changed as a result of this calamity. Yet, had our mythical Jones been practicing for some time the techniques we are discussing, the crisis might have been completely averted.

By taking into account all of his audiences, especially the various segments of the local community, Jones might have developed the credibility and community support needed to cause people to think twice before lashing out.

It can make a big difference. Let's indulge in a little revisionist history.

DEDMETE INDUSTRIES: A CASE STUDY (PART II)

Sam Jones parks his Mercedes and walks to the office complex. As he crosses the parking lot, he waves at the team of archaeology students from the local college who are excavating a small section of the plant property in search of native American artifacts. Jones welcomes the publicity the company is receiving from the project and has offered to fund a traveling exhibition of any object found on the site.

As Jones walks into his handsomely paneled office, his secretary, Ms. Debote, greets him and tells him that Mr. Skull and Ms. Crossbones of the Environmental Protection Agency called to request an appointment to discuss an urgent matter, about which they had written to him several weeks previously. Jones knows all about it—his lawyers have already reviewed the letter and are prepared to cooperate since Dedmete is in full compliance with the EPA's guidelines.

Jones checks his calendar: He has a meeting with the chairman of the local consumer activist group scheduled for Friday. At that time he will reveal his decision to make, once again, a substantial contribution to the group, which he encourages his employees to join. He also could use the meeting to discuss the EPA case and Dedmete's intention to help ensure that the local water supply is of top quality. He instructs Ms. Debote to set up the meeting with the EPA for Thursday afternoon.

Next, Jones calls the Mayor's office. When he first received the letter from the EPA, he called the Mayor to express his alarm concerning the possible endangerment of the local water supply and to assure His Honor that Dedmete was not involved in any contamination. However, because his employees and their families drink the water, Jones offered the town technical and financial assistance to help track down the problem and locate the guilty parties. Today, Jones suggests that the Mayor's and Dedmete's public relations staffs meet to discuss how best to handle any press inquiries (Jones knows the Mayor is up for reelection this year and is looking for opportunities to look smart). The Mayor agrees and tells him how much he's looking forward to the Junior Achievement dinner next week.

Finally, Jones calls the Right Reverend Hy N. Mighty to see if he has had the chance to think about Jones's offer to set up a committee on the homeless, with the Rt. Reverend as chairman. The Rt. Reverend is delighted and says he looks forward to seeing Jones and his family on Sunday.

It's now 10:00 A.M. Smith calls—he has awarded Dedmete the big contract and wonders if Jones is free for a round of golf this afternoon.

Okay, this scenario may be a trifle Pollyanna-esque, but it's certainly true that the support of the local community can make a crucial difference in how you fare in a crisis. It is worth your time and trouble to build bridges to key constituents who may have more public credibility than you do when a crisis erupts. That's why managing your impact on the community is so important.

Normally, the effort you must devote to community relations depends on the degree to which the community is affected by your company's presence. Large companies typically have greater positive and negative impacts upon the community than small ones. For example, on the "asset" side, large manufacturing operations employ more people, contribute more money to the local tax base, and typically have more money to give to local charities than small manufacturing operations have.

On the "liability" side, the larger companies also typically produce greater quantities of waste, sometimes hazardous. Their operations often cause greater increases in traffic, especially big truck traffic, than small companies do.

Rest assured, someone is keeping a running total on the assets and liabilities, and the positives had better far outweigh the negatives, for your sake.

'Twas not ever thus. It used to be that if your company was the largest employer in town, you could do pretty much whatever you wanted. Nobody questioned whether you were acting in the long-term interests of the community— it was assumed that you were by virtue of the fact that you gave a man a job in the same factory where his father had worked and would be there again when his son graduated (or left) high school. That was enough. If anyone wondered about the hundreds of gallons of foul-smelling effluent that the factory dumped into the river every day, nothing much was said. If the once-legendary vista of the neighboring mountains was obscured by billowing black clouds of smoke from the factory's stacks, that was the price of progress.

Today, that price is a bit too steep for most people, and all companies—regardless of their size—are expected to be "good citizens." A vigilant corps of whistle-blowers will remind you when, in their eyes, you fail to do so. As we suggested in our opening scenario, this is a force to be reckoned with because in extreme situations they can shut you down. There is no question but that it pays to maintain your credibility with these watchdogs before they get too upset about something.

That "something" may not even be your problem, per se. Subsidiaries can become the object of opprobrium because of the activities of the parent, and vice versa. The actions of a distant relative can besmirch the entire family name, as was made clear to American Express when its investment banking subsidiary, Shearson/American Express, was retained by a British firm, Beazer P.L.C., to bankroll the takeover of Koppers, a Pennsylvania company. Although Shearson acts independently from American Express, the parent company was more than a little dismayed to see Koppers employees destroying their American Express credit cards on the six o'clock news. Dow Chemical's freezer bags are made by a different division than are the chemicals used in napalm, but because there was no way to boycott napalm use, activists shunned the bags. Boycotts may be coordinated on a national level, but the decision to participate remains rooted at the local level.

Still, most companies with community problems can't blame them on a parent company or a subsidiary, and in any case, no matter where the blame lies, the problem remains a local one. An ongoing community relations program will help to identify potential problems before they turn your company into "Dedmete Industries."

AUDIT THE COMMUNITY

As is the case with many of the subjects touched upon in this book, community relations is deserving of an entire book unto itself—in fact, from our perspective, it is central to the process of managing corporate impact. Nowhere can the effects of such management (or lack of it) be felt greater than in your own community.

As we might recommend before undertaking any communications program, an audit is the most effective first step you can take toward better community relations. Start by examining the obvious points of impact your company has on the community, both positive and negative.

If your company is the largest in town, that probably means you provide employment to a significant number of local residents. That's a plus, obviously. That same fact, however, also may mean that your company's operations cause a significant increase in heavy-vehicle traffic over what would otherwise be present—which creates a substantial burden on local roads, may sometimes cause traffic tie-ups, and may also contribute to a reduction in overall air quality.

You may be bringing substantial quantities of chemicals onto the site. More importantly, you may be emitting chemicals into the environment (legally or otherwise). These factors are of concern to everyone—employees, their families, and other town residents.

Some additional "internal" concerns include the fiscal health of the company; the state of labor relations; concessions, such as tax breaks or incentives the company has received from the town; and the degree to which these matters affect other companies in the area (i.e., has your company received really special treatment?).

External factors to keep in mind include the political environment. Is it stable, or are there key offices in contention? Has your company or any other company in town been the subject of scrutiny by local legislators or media? Are there any community activists based in the area (don't forget about religious groups)? Is there a local chapter of a major environmentalist group, such as the Sierra Club?

These are just some of the factors you need to take into consideration when analyzing your community. The next step is to review your internal procedures (if any exist) for handling inquiries or complaints from the community and for staying abreast of the issues that are of greatest concern to the local population.

For instance, is there a person designated as the community relations officer? Are records kept of all inquiries and complaints, along with copies of replies? Does anyone monitor the issues of possible concern to the town: rapid growth, drug abuse, homelessness, and teenage pregnancy as well as concerns specific to the local community? Does a company representative attend town meetings?

Finally, what activities does the company sponsor or initiate in order to foster good community relations? Typical examples include:

- attendance at Rotary Club meetings
- membership in the local Chamber of Commerce and attendance at its meetings
- organization of the United Way campaign within the company

- sponsorship of a blood drive at the company
- offering of plant tours to school and other interested groups.

As a responsive strategy, the idea is to be sensitive to the concerns of the community, in general and about your company specifically, and to demonstrate that sensitivity through action. At the same time, you can undertake a variety of activities designed to generate goodwill without becoming pegged to specific issues or concerns. For example, you may wish to donate goods or services to help rebuild a school after a fire, even though education per se is not one of your target issues.

So far, we've focused on community relations as a means of attaining and preserving goodwill in your local community. It is also sometimes necessary to initiate community relations tactics in other communities. For instance, if you are planning to relocate to another town, it pays to begin the community relations process well in advance of the move. Even if you are a so-called desirable company, bringing lots of good jobs and little environmental impact, you may still need to establish ties to the new community early on—to facilitate zoning changes or to secure preferential tax treatment, for example. If yours is a manufacturing facility, contact with the community early and often is advised, as Puremotiva learned.

PUREMOTIVA INDUSTRIES

Some stereotypes die very hard. For example, it is accepted wisdom that left-handed pitchers are flaky, taxes always go up under the Democrats, and all chemical plants are smelly. And if it's a paper-processing chemical plant, it must be smelly *and dirty*.

The management of Puremotiva Products knew better. They had developed a technology that could take a spray of woodchips and crush, pummel, squeeze, soak, sluice, boil, press, twist, pound, and push them into pretty little cardboard boxes with nary an odor escaping the cauldron. All the bilious green effluence could be treated, piped underground, and released many miles away where nobody would ever see it.

It was determined that a new plant would be built to house the revolutionary new process. The Puremotiva pooh-bahs scouted out and snatched up an attractive location that seemed perfect: It was near their source of supply and the community was a seasonal resort town where their plant managers would like to live and where Puremotiva top brass would like to visit. The company hired the best local law firm, whose senior partner was the current Mayor, to secure the necessary variances and town permission, and they started to break ground.

It was fall in the upper peninsula resort city of Wolverton, on the pristine shore of upper Lake Michigan, and most of the "summer" people had departed. The permanent residents watched with some curiosity as the big factory buildings started to take shape. It was rumored that the building shells would be enclosed before the winter snows so that completion could be scheduled for the spring.

Then one day a curious reporter from the weekly Wolverton *Eagle-Express-News* engaged a plant construction foreman in idle conversation over a few beers at Mama's Watering Hole.

"What sort of factory are you building out there on East Lake Street?"

"Oh, a processing plant."

"What's gonna be processed there?"

"Don't you know?"

"No. Nobody's said."

"Paperboard. Paper boxes."

"Wow. I thought it was some advanced technology stuff."

"Naw. Lot of new equipment. But paper stuff is what comes out."

That Friday morning the headline on the front page of the eight-page *Eagle-Express-News* told of the giant paper-processing factory that was going to dominate the eastern shore of Wolverton's lakefront. Along with it ran an artist's rendering of the plant's possible shape, complete with four smokestacks belching thickly billowing smoke. A sidebar on the chemical waste produced by paper plants and released untreated into local waterways featured a photograph of Cleveland's Cuyahoga River during the sixties, when its surface would actually catch fire.

Though the story also told of 600 new jobs that would be created and detailed descriptions of the marvelously versatile cluster-pack boxes the plant would turn out for shipment throughout the Midwest, the talk all over town that weekend was of the black smoke and the likely effect on the beachfronts.

"The beautiful resort of Wolverton will soon look and smell like Cleveland!" was the most frequently heard sentiment in the local churches that Sunday.

By Monday petitions were being readied, and "Save Our Air" and "Keep Our Beaches Clean for Our Grandchildren" committees were being formed. The Ladies Thursday Bridge Club was checking the bus schedules to Lansing, the state capital.

In the days that followed, while the building of the factory proceeded apace, petitions to forbid the opening of the plant were circulated in every barbershop, supermarket, and restaurant in town. Letters and telephone calls to the local congressman multiplied, and a suit to enjoin the opening of the factory was filed with the district state court. One group was also organizing an action to circle the plant site with placard-carrying citizens, demanding a halt to construction.

By now top management of the Puremotiva Company in Youngstown, Ohio, had begun to take notice of what those "crazy people up in Michigan" were doing.

"Tell them what we're going to do for that rotten burg," said the president to his first senior executive vice president. "Tell them we're bringing in 600 new jobs that won't disappear every fall. Show them what we'll give them in taxes for their roads and schools in that city of 12,000. And tell them our plant won't emit one lousy odor! And there won't be any smoke! And we'll pipe all the crap way downstream where their precious beaches will never be affected."

The president was being restrained by his colleagues now.

"Take it easy, boss. How should we tell them?"

"How the hell do I know? Take out ads. Go on television. Do it with skywriting. How do I know? Ask the pros."

Alas, emotions in the community had already outrun the "pros." Puremotiva should have explained its plans to the community before it started to build. The declining economy of Wolverton would surely have been helped by the new industry. Though chemicals and paper-processing factories conjure up dire pictures in the minds of most people, this one would truly have controlled the effluences. Its architecture would have blended in reasonably well with its section of town, and it would not have affected the quality or appearance of the beaches.

But nobody at Puremotiva thought to discuss it first with the people most affected and listen to their concerns and fears. They just forged ahead, confident that they knew best, leaving themselves vulnerable to the community's deepest paranoia about callous outsiders.

It is now years later. The sullen, boarded-up shell of the never-completed Puremotiva factory building is being looked at by condo developers as the centerpiece of their "new age lifestyle center" (a glorified indoor tennis and hockey facility). Trouble is, there isn't anybody in Wolverton who can afford to invest in the condos. They're being marketed to Southfield yuppies as second homes.

Somebody at Mama's Watering Hole had an idea. "Maybe those guys from Ohio, remember them? Maybe they'd like to start some sort of subsidiary. . . ."

* * *

If you think you've got your hands full keeping up your image in your local community as well as in the community you're expanding to, remember that saying goodbye is never easy, either. In some states—New Jersey, for one—you may have to have an active community relations program in towns where you currently have no presence at all—but once did. State environmental laws increasingly hold companies responsible for site contamination even after the property has changed hands. In some cases, states are empowered to nullify the sale years after the fact in order to force the previous owner to clean up the site.

Growing more typical these days are the concessions companies have to make when they shut down operations in a particular community. As Chrysler and other companies have recently learned, the cost of shutting down a plant may have to include maintaining the payroll for an extended period, funding job training programs, selling the plant site at a loss to encourage another company to buy it, and even retrofitting the plant for a new type of business. Even more painful: If the local community has granted special tax breaks as an incentive to keep you in town and you announce that you plan to pull up stakes, you could be on the hook to repay those special benefits.

8

Standing Out on Wall Street

From Going Public to Staying Independent to Being Taken Over

Chapter 8

On October 19, 1987, "a date which will live in infamy" (to borrow the words of a depression-era U.S. president), the Dow Jones Average of 30 Industrials took a figurative step off a window ledge and fell over 500 points before it splattered on Wall Street. In the wake of the crash, stock watchers have replaced their Maalox with Dramamine as the Average alternately climbs and plummets like a Learjet in a snowstorm.

Prior to the crash, new stock issues seemed to come forth almost daily as closely held companies sought to cash in on the unprecedented bull market that raged over the previous four years or so.

It seemed that going public was a practically risk-free proposition—issue the stock, someone would buy it. These issues were carried along with the rest of the market until the price–earnings ratios were far in excess of what traditional market theory would have supported just half a decade before.

In the postcrash era, it's clear that going public will no longer be so easy. Investors are very careful with their money these days, and a company contemplating an initial public offering (IPO) had better keep in mind the story about the man and the talking bird. It seems the man walked into a very classy pet shop and bought what was advertised as a talking bird. The bird was tenderly and carefully crated and brought home.

The next day, the customer showed up at the pet shop and buttonholed the owner.

"Bird don't talk," he said.

Expressing his surprise, the owner said, "Perhaps the bird's not getting enough exercise. Here, why don't you buy this nice trapeze. It'll enable him to swing."

The next day, the customer returned.

"Bird don't talk," he said again.

"Heavens!" exclaimed the shop owner. "Perhaps he doesn't feel clean. Take this birdbath and ladder and place it in his cage. It will enable him to refresh himself."

This the customer did, only to return the next day.

"Bird still don't talk."

Ths shop owner was desperate, but maintaining his composure, suggested that the bird might be lonely.

"Take these mirrors and put them around the cage. Perhaps the bird will think he has company and start talking."

The customer took the mirrors and left. Days passed with no sign of the customer, until one day by chance the owner came upon the man on the street.

"Well, sir," he said. "How's your talking bird these days?"

"Bird died," was the reply.

Horrified, the shop owner said, "That's a terrible shame. But tell me, did he ever talk?"

"Just before he died," the man said. "Turned his head and said, 'Doesn't that damn pet shop sell birdseed?'"

As people up and down Wall Street are being reminded every day, you can't overlook the basics.

GOING PUBLIC

There are any number of reasons why you might wish to become a publicly traded company. Most have to do with money, of course. Large-scale expansion plans or the need for extensive research and development funds are two of the most common reasons.

The process of undertaking an initial public offering is complicated and requires the services of many professionals, including lawyers and bankers. Increasingly, the importance of the communications counselor is becoming more widely known.

Communications play an essential role in the process of "going public" that is often overlooked. Many managers understand the need for investor relations *after* the initial public offering, but not enough place importance on communications *before* the offering—preferably well before it. As is true with most elements of the IPO process, these communications can be complicated to organize and manage. It makes a lot of sense to engage a public relations firm with experience in such things. But even when you leave communications to professionals, you should know what steps must be taken and why, if only so you know what kind of time and effort you'll be committing yourself to. Let's take a closer look at these activities.

When your company becomes a publicly traded corporation, you add a very important new product to your line: stock. In order for your IPO to be successful, you have to convince the investing public that your stock is a good product. What makes a stock a good product is whatever meets the investor's needs. Investors look for growth, income, or a combination of both. You have to show that your stock will offer one or more of those attributes. While doing so does not guarantee a successful offering, failing to do so means the offering will surely fail, too.

The criteria investors will use to gauge the merit of your stock will be familiar to you: past earnings history, strength and depth of management, market share and marketing strategy, product or service quality, and uniqueness—all of the things by which you measure a successful business.

The key is to begin communicating this data early. As much as a year prior to the offering, a product publicity and corporate visibility campaign should be initiated. The objective is to create awareness of your company before you go public. Then, when your stock begins trading, investors and analysts will already know who and what you are and can focus their attention on the particulars of the offering.

Remember, you are not a public company yet. The most contact you can hope for with the analysts who follow your industry is to add them to your press mailing list. (Use some discretion about the type and quantity of items you send. Minor personnel announcements will only annoy them. Stick to what would be "material" information for a public company.)

Other than this first step, the only way to reach the Wall Street gang (and potential investors) is through the media. Initiate a publicity program designed to reach key business/financial media with information about your company. Focus on past performance and aspects of the company's business that will contribute to growth and profitability. You'll also want to demonstrate management's stability and control.

Communicating to Wall Street is vital, but it is equally important to identify those cities in the United States and abroad that are essential to your company. Develop a list of electronic media, newspapers, and business and trade magazines to include on your press materials distribution list.

Look for speaking opportunities that provide a forum for a "philosophical" speech relating to the changing world of your industry. The text of the speech can be included in press materials and helps to underscore your credibility.

Meanwhile, your lawyers and bankers will have plenty of other things for you to do. As you approach the registration period, your days are going to get very busy. Too bad, because you've still got to run a business and run it well. At last, after all your press interviews, your bylined articles, and your speeches, you get to that magic day that begins what's called the "quiet period," a 180-day "hiatus" beginning exactly 90 days prior to the offering and continuing 90 days after. Thank heavens, a chance to rest your weary jaw, right? Not quite.

The Quiet Period

We'll always remember the day we received a call from a client with whom we had undertaken several projects. We were stunned by her news: Although we were in the midst of an assignment, effective immediately, we were fired.

When we pressed for a reason, she was reluctant to give one, and (even more mysteriously) instead spoke of how much she had enjoyed working with us and how pleased she had been with our results.

Finally, we told her that it was simply unfair of her to terminate us without some explanation. After a moment, she said, "We're going public, and we are in the quiet period." She even spoke quietly—indeed, she just about whispered.

It took a lot of back and forth with her and the company's lawyers before we were able to disabuse them of the notion that "quiet" equals "silence." Quite the opposite is true. The main concern of the SEC is that you do not actively tout the stock in your communications. In general terms, the SEC encourages you to *maintain the current level* of communications. For starters, go ahead and continue your marketing communications. No investor will be served if you stop and, by doing so, lose market share for your products. Continue to seek general profiles of your company and business and trade media—just be careful not to talk about the impending public offering.

That's where the SEC gets a little touchy. Communications activities pertaining to the public offering are very much prescribed by law and center around two major events: preparation of the registration statement/prospectus and the road show.

The prospectus has two potentially conflicting objectives: Under the Securities Act of 1933, it must provide complete disclosure, revealing negative as well as positive aspects of the company. At the same time, it is the basic sales brochure for the stock issue and should present the best possible company image. The resulting document is at best unexciting.

The Road Show

It is the road show that provides a company with the chance to create an initial favorable impression and generate immediate investor interest. While these meetings theoretically are intended to allow the professionals to study company operations and investment potential at close range, they also offer management an excellent opportunity to exhibit strong leadership and emphasize the stability and viability of operations.

That first impression is critical because professionals draw conclusions from the material presented as well as how management demonstrates its ability, knowledge, and familiarity with industry trends.

In addition to describing operations, the presentation should clearly position the company and its competitive advantages. It should also express management's philosophy and outlook for growth (this is touchy—you must be sure to stay within the limits of SEC regulations on projections).

Outline your financial strategies, especially your capital spending plans. Tell investors how you intend to use their money. Be sure to present your marketing plan, including public relations and advertising.

Being careful not to create unrealistic expectations, use the road show to sell your company to the people who influence the buyers.

While SEC regulations clearly limit direct communications on the part of the company during this period, you can employ some interesting supplemental tactics, especially with your customer base. For example, if your company operates a chain of retail outlets, you can produce display cards for the checkout counters that announce your impending offering and encourage customers to get hold of a prospectus. Mail-order firms can accomplish the same thing with catalog inserts.

However, because we are on the edge of SEC regulations, it's essential to be conservative and to make sure that any ideas and copy are approved by the lawyers. The SEC still limits many of these efforts. For example, they stipulate that the information used in other vehicles be limited to what is in the printed prospectuses. And in some cases, they have limited distribution to brokers, excluding the general public.

During the post-offering 90 days of the quiet period, it's a good time to develop the material needed for the investor relations program, which we'll discuss in detail later. Use this hiatus to develop guidelines, programs, and information needed for analyst contact. Decide on the types and extent of investor literature and designate who is responsible for its development and distribution. Develop a mechanism for handling financial media communications, including writing and distributing press releases and responding to inquiries from the financial press.

Okay, that's a theoretical primer. Let's look at two notable examples of what we're talking about. Both concern savings banks, and before starting, we should note that banks are not entirely comparable to other enterprises because they are not as strictly bound by the Securities Act of 1933 with regard to the quiet period. Still, those differences notwithstanding, the cases are good examples of how communications can make the difference.

Anchor Savings Bank, headquartered in Hewlett, Long Island, was founded in 1838 as a New York state-chartered mutual savings bank. In 1980, Anchor converted to a federally chartered mutual savings bank. Over the years, Anchor had been aggressive in originating mortgages, acquiring other savings institutions, and, to the extent allowed by law, developing banking operations in other states. In 1986, Anchor announced that it planned to convert from a mutual savings bank to a publicly owned company to enable it to expand its out-of-state banking operations and its burgeoning national presence in mortgage originations.

Anchor had some distinct advantages over other banks in terms of going public, most notably its already widespread public recognition. Donald Thomas, the bank's longtime chairman, had for years been appearing with his wife Barbara in the bank's television and newspaper advertisements. Viewers throughout the New York metropolitan area were extremely familiar with the signature line appearing in each ad: (He says) "Your Anchor Banker . . . he understands!" (She says) "That's right . . . Your Anchor Banker . . . *she* understands!"

Anchor had also done a good job of managing its impact on a variety of audiences: It was active in civic affairs and took a genuine interest in the communities in which it had branches. The bank was a leader in the effort to develop affordable housing in low- and middle-income neighborhoods, and Don Thomas was personally involved in many charitable causes.

Because mutual companies are in essence "owned" by their customers, depositors and borrowers are entitled to first crack at buying newly issued stock. Therefore, customers were allowed to subscribe to the offering in advance of the stock issuance. Furthermore, anyone who lived in a neighborhood served by a branch of the bank was eligible to subscribe in advance.

Because of the need to alert these potential investors to this opportunity, Anchor was allowed to aggressively market the fact that it was going public. A television campaign was launched—the ever-familiar Thomases announced, "We're going public," and invited viewers to stop by any Anchor branch and get in on the action.

These ads were supplemented by an ambitious series of road shows, both domestically and abroad. The Anchor management team met with analysts and brokers several times a day for several weeks, outlining the bank's strong history, marketing plans, and business strategy.

Articles featuring the stock conversion, with a focus on Anchor management, were developed for major banking and financial trade publications. Newspapers around the state hailed the impending stock issue as a chance for the small investor to get in on something big.

Anchor Customers . . . they understood.

Reports of customers waltzing into branches and buying thousands of dollars of stock began to surface. In a matter of weeks, the subscription was sold out—in fact, it was oversubscribed. It was the most successful subscription anyone could recall, certainly in banking circles.

Anchor management was jubilant. Salomon Brothers, Anchor's underwriter, was depressed. It had been assumed that a significant portion of the stock would not be sold through the subscription, and Salomon had planned to earn a substantial commission on aftermarket sales. Indeed, these commissions were to pay for their time and expenses in actually preparing, underwriting, and administering the conversion process. Now they were in the rather awkward position of having to negotiate compensation for their out-of-pocket expenses.

All of this sounds terrific for Anchor, but the story isn't all rosy: Although the stock sold out at the subscription price of $11.50 per share and rose a point or two after the initial listing (leaving some observers to wonder if it had been underpriced), it dropped a point almost immediately . . . then another and another. For several months after the listing, the stock price languished at around $10.00. Or, perhaps it simply defied gravity.

The truth is that the stock was probably well-priced at the range of $8.50 to $11.50 per share that had been calculated by Salomon Brothers, a range based on assets and liabilities—the book value—and projected earnings. The stock could be expected to sell reasonably well, but nothing like the way it actually did.

What made the difference was communications. Anchor did such a good job of capitalizing on its existing identity within its service areas that people felt they were practically investing in the family business. Had Anchor been an obscure savings bank with little prior name recognition, the offering probably would have been less dramatic and perhaps quite tepid. That name recognition allowed communications efforts to focus on the offering itself, instead of on establishing an identity for the bank.

With the tumult of October 1987, the stock fell dramatically, as did most stocks, but over time it began to show steady improvement. Communications continued to play a role—a strong investor relations program ultimately helped support the stock price. Although later, the share-price gradually descended in line with the stocks of other thrifts, overall, the offering has been considered a success.

It was especially deemed so in contrast to the disappointing results experienced by Goldome, which undertook an offering in virtually the same region and within three months of the Anchor conversion.

Goldome, an even bigger thrift headquartered in Buffalo, had grown dramatically in previous years through the acquisition of other banks around the state. Goldome had only become a factor in the New York City area in the past five or six years with its acquisition of a couple of major New York savings institutions.

Thus, in New York, from which a major proportion of investors would be drawn, Goldome had 6 years of exposure, as opposed to Anchor's nearly 150 years. Even if one assumes that Anchor's identity was greatly expanded by its television ads, it still had decades of exposure compared to Goldome's handful of years.

Then, too, Goldome had not been acting in a manner designed to inspire confidence in its management. Originally a state-chartered institution, Goldome had determined, like Anchor, that it would be better off as a federally chartered bank—and had converted. Then, within an embarrassingly short time, it changed its mind, and a scant few months before announcing its intention to go public, switched back, leaving heads spinning among industry analysts.

Anxious to lure investment dollars to fund expansion, and undoubtedly spurred on by Anchor's success, Goldome undertook a major media blitz to draw potential investors into Goldome branches. Like Anchor, Goldome ran television ads, but they did not have the Thomases' friendly faces in them. They ran newspaper ads, but they were not personality-driven like Anchor's.

In the end, Goldome was able to move only 40 percent of its stock in subscription at the low end of its range and is reported to have spent several million dollars to do it.

Even without attempting to compare and critique the specific merits and faults of Goldome's road show, ads, and publicity efforts as compared to Anchor's, there is one conclusion that is inescapable. Anchor's long-established identity as a stable, friendly institution gave it the credibility it needed when it went public.

Even though, as banks, Anchor and Goldome are in different circumstances than most companies looking to undertake an initial public offering, the lesson here should not be ignored. Spend the time it takes to become a known and respected company within your industry and in your own backyard *before* you even think about an offering—it will pay off.

INVESTOR RELATIONS

But what if your company has been publicly owned for many years and its stock is languishing. You feel it is a good company with good prospects. In today's barracuda-infested waters, you are concerned that if the stock price doesn't get healthier, some raider will spot you and come after you.

What should you do? First, you must have a story to tell.

Wall Street needs an "investable idea." With thousands of stocks available on a dozen different exchanges, investors are always on the prowl for what's new and different . . . or more likely, what will be new and different in 18 months, something that will drive up the price of the stock and provide some handsome dividends.

Look deep down into the bowels of your company and see if you can find some unique product on its way through your research department. If not, then how about a fortuitously repositioned product to capitalize on a change in consumer demand? Other possible themes: a new management team coming in with new strategic plans; a hot new niche acquisition that will make your major line of business much more competitive; a new process that will substantially lower your production or distribution costs; a charismatic new chief executive officer joining from a highly respected company. All of these story lines will be attractive to one or another segment of the investor universe.

The next step is to examine your standard communications techniques to see if they can be improved. Use your corporate annual report to explain your lines of business better. Each of your quarterly reports can highlight a different segment of your business. You could develop a fact book for analysts that would make it easier for them to understand and explain your company.

You should develop through your internal public relations director or outside public relations counsel a closer relationship with the major business publications. An occasional Dow-Jones exclusive interview with your CEO, wherein he or she discusses expected earnings patterns and new developments in the company and the industry, can draw additional attention from the *Wall Street Journal* and get investors and analysts noticing your firm.

Other special features in such publications as *Business Week*, *Forbes*, and *Fortune* would be desirable. *Financial World, Inc.* and *Industry Week* are also good. You can magnify the impact of a favorable story by reprinting it and mailing it to selected analysts and fund managers who may have missed it.

The leading trade publications in each of your industries are also worth cultivating. The more astute analysts follow these magazines assiduously, hoping to get a jump on other financial advisors or at least keep from falling behind.

While it is accepted wisdom that inefficient valuations of stock usually result when there's an information gap on the part of investors, you have to bear in mind that along with the press, security analysts are the primary interpreters of that information. These analysts work for institutions who process that information according to their own particular philosophies.

Among the more common institutional investment approaches are the following:

- Value-oriented—looks for companies with high-quality earnings and strong market potential not yet recognized by most of Wall Street. Judgments are not yet made on the basis of the earnings stream but on the underlying values that can generate future earnings.
- Contrarian—looks for out-of-favor industries and companies with sound fundamentals that are perceived to be misunderstood by the market.
- Emerging Growth—attracted to small companies likely to produce unusual growth because they have developed a very innovative product or are in a market segment that is beginning to get a lot of attention.
- Misperceived Stocks—looks for stocks that have changed but are still seen by the general marketplace in old stereotypical ways.
- Fundamentalist—forms opinions based on the classic Graham and Dodd analytical approach: basic balance-sheet dividend stream approach that is in keeping with the inherent strengths of the company.

Then there are the Sector Rotation investment counselors, the market timers, the Top Down'ers and the Bottom Up'ers. And of course, we mustn't forget the newest scourge, the Program Traders.

Don't try to outguess any of these heroic market pundits.

Just try to put your company's best foot forward with the objective of achieving the highest sustainable price.

Remember, too, that while you are struggling to create a unique identity for your company among investors, don't be afraid to draw comparisons between your company and another. For example, it is quite helpful to an analyst if you can say that your company is "rather like XYZ except we have targeted a different market segment. . . . " Make sure the company you compare yourself to is also a winner. What the heck, be optimistic and enthusiastic. Analysts like that kind of drive. Just don't get carried away and compare yourself to IBM, unless you happen to be Digital.

Perhaps the most egregious offense a company can perpetrate in its investor relations is to surprise the analysts who follow the company. Most typically, this comes in the form of the issuance of quarterly earnings results well below analysts' expectations.

During the quarter, analysts make estimates as to what they believe your earnings per share will be. Some will even call you to see if their estimates seem reasonable to you. If you believe that these estimates are accurate, by all means so indicate. On the other hand, if you think the estimates are way off the mark—too high or even too low—it will behoove you to enlighten the analyst as soon as possible.

If you don't correct the situation, the announcement of your earnings will be the one thing analysts hate most of all: a surprise. At this point, the current volatility in the stock market provides all the surprises any but the most substance-abusing analyst could want. Why add to the confusion? If you have taken the trouble to make clear the reasons why you expect earnings to be off a bit in the current quarter, the eventual announcement will be expected and its overall impact will have already been factored in by the time you release the official results. In spite of repeated evidence supporting this tactic, many executives still live on the hope that a last-minute miracle will allow them to pull a rabbit out of the hat.

The government is one of the worst offenders employing this head-in-the-sand strategy, by the way. As a case in point, consider the April 14, 1988 announcement of the monthly trade deficit figures. Economists were expecting good news: a decline in the deficit. The actual figures were stunning: a $2.5 billion increase! In the first half-hour of trading, the Dow lost 30 points as inflationary fears and talk of higher interest rates propelled the market. The closing bell saw a total decline of more than 100 points.

One cynical wag has suggested that the Reagan Administration's unwillingness to soften the blow in advance might just have been a crude attempt to manage its impact: With several major electoral primaries underway around the country in the weeks prior to the announcement, the erroneous optimism was strategically advantageous to the Republican party. In the long run, of course, it had just the opposite effect.

Tactical Investor Relations

Because of the domino-like effect of corporate impact, investor relations can be leveraged to accomplish a larger goal. The recently ended Pennzoil–Texaco debacle is a case in point.

Remember the basic facts: Pennzoil wanted to buy Getty Oil and reached an agreement with Getty to do so. Texaco, suddenly aware of Getty's value, made a better offer to Getty, and Getty reneged on its agreement with Pennzoil.

A Texas jury sided with Pennzoil and found that Texaco had done Pennzoil wrong. The Texas Supreme Court later upheld both the decision and the record-setting damages awarded to Pennzoil.

Despite repeated losses in court, Texaco skillfully portrayed itself as the victim. The company entered bankruptcy proceedings as a defensive measure to prevent having to pay the damages, and many observers questioned whether Pennzoil would ever collect a dime. After two and a half years of letting the courts do the talking, Pennzoil turned to its public relations agency for help.

The agency's counsel, among other things, was to examine what was being said to the analyst community. Since Texaco was seen as an international oil company while Pennzoil was viewed as strictly domestic, the two companies were followed by different analysts. The Texaco analysts were only hearing the Texaco story.

An analyst meeting was scheduled—for Texaco analysts. Whereas an analyst meeting usually features the company's CEO and CFO, this meeting was different. On hand to speak to the analysts were several experts on the constitutional issues involved in the case. The meeting was almost exclusively devoted to explaining why Pennzoil's case against Texaco was so strong.

After a day to digest the presentation, the analysts spoke out. Many were quoted as saying that until the Pennzoil analyst meeting, they never understood just how shaky Texaco's case was. Pennzoil stock jumped more than two points, while Texaco stock declined. The sudden bearish view of Texaco was the first chink in the company's armor. Major investors, deprived of dividends while Texaco was in Chapter 11 and seeing the tide turning against the company, pressured Texaco for a settlement. For the first time, Pennzoil was perceived to be the likely winner. Within 90 days, a settlement was announced.

LBOS AND MBOS: FYI

Back in the 1960s, astute financial managers were falling all over themselves to acquire companies. It was the era of conglomeration, and size was the goal. Grab the companies and fold them in, by friendly, semi-friendly, or out-and-out hostile means.

The accumulation of diverse and disparate companies into a monumental enterprise with a distinctive and descriptive name, such as United Amalgamation Industries, was the action, and the buzzword for creating shareholder values was *synergy*. One plus one equals three: The diverse companies, thrown together in one large pot, would somehow help each other grow faster by rubbing their special knowledges off on each other.

The stock market seemed to buy that story, too. Share prices of many of the loosely related, often ill-conceived, multi-industry assemblages soared. That enabled the astute financial manager to acquire even more companies.

But gradually, more cool-headed analysts began to point out that bottom-line figures were not keeping pace with the top-line numbers. And so "conglomeratization" ran out of steam. Even the word *conglomerate* fell into disfavor. The astute financial manager scurried to rearrange his or her holdings to show how they fit some brilliant grand design.

Today the action has come about smartly, heading in the opposite direction from whence it came. Value for shareholders seems to be best obtained through divestment of divisions and subsidiaries. Companies buy from other companies to share their strengths rather than enter new fields of combat.

But you also hear a lot about "going private." That usually means a leveraged buy out (LBO), where investors, often with the cooperation of divisional management, borrow most of the money to buy the business and hope to pay off the usually staggering debt with the cash flow of the new company. When the divisional or subsidiary management are part of the deal it is referred to as a management buy out, or MBO.

A whole stratum of financial advisers has sprouted to structure these deals. Kohlberg, Kravis, & Roberts (KKR), Forstmann Little, and Conniston Partners are among the best known. They work closely with investment banks and those commercial banks who are now getting into the fast-paced action.

What this is all about is making money. But it has the further redeeming characteristic of giving the managers a chance to run their own business—the American Dream. Instead of the giant conglomerate in the role of overlord, however, substitute that of money changer. Payments must be made promptly.

Still, former corporate managers now become entrepreneurs who know that although they will pay for failures, they will also be better rewarded for successes.

LBOs had been picking up in momentum through the late seventies and the eighties, but recently they have burst to the fore. This occurred when the management buy-out concept was applied to the purchase of large, publicly owned companies, often as an alternative to a hostile takeover. It is a way for managers to preserve their jobs and keep their company from being dismembered by outsiders. Of course, the debt may get so great—or the temptation of huge potential personal rewards so staggering—that managers may be lead to dismember the company themselves.

The biggest negative in an LBO or MBO is the huge debt that is incurred. Sometimes this new debt is piled on top of an already debt-laden company, which can bring things to the brink of bankruptcy if all does not go well.

On the plus side, there is the incentive that the managers develop as they realize they own the place. They work harder, waste less, and concern themselves less with the trappings of office (such as private planes, limousines, hunting lodges, etc.) and more with the real essentials of productivity.

Also, as a private company, the managers are not forced into the quarterly earnings rat race. If a quarter or two show a drop in revenue, it is not the end of the world. They can plan for longer term growth. And they can give valued staff bigger pieces of the action.

Developing communications plans for an LBO is not all

that difficult. It's easy to identify the strengths and weaknesses of most LBOs. On the negative side, the potential investors backing the buy out need to feel secure that the crushing debt can be borne by the new company long enough for the sale of assets and the existing cash flow to whittle it down. These same investors will also want to know that the proposed new management under which the company will be operated are competent and not remembered best for a major failure of the past.

The strengths: Ah, well, one need only show the color of one's money. The Wall Street gang will always welcome a chance to tender their stock for a significant premium. Let your checkbook do the talking.

We are talking about friendly deals here. Of course, there is always the possibility that the current management will not look upon your attempts to maximize shareholder value with the same enthusiasm as you do—after all, the very act of initiating an LBO sort of assumes that you believe that you can do a better job of running the company than the existing management. If that's the case, then we should look at hostile takeovers because that's what an unfriendly deal amounts to.

THE TAKEOVER GAME

Like baseball and basketball, the takeover is a game invented in America but spreading fast to other parts of the world. There are clear and immediate winners and losers in this game, too. But the effects don't end on any grassy diamond or hardwood court. They reach down through all levels of society and shake the cores of publicly and privately held companies. Whole communities are changed, the economies of cities and states can be altered. It is the publicly owned companies, though, that are on the front line.

* * *

It had been a great day for Sam Jones, coming at the end of a week of accomplishment. Jones, president of Dedmete Industries, had spent the morning going over his advertising agency's recommendations for a new campaign. The TV spots looked great. After the presentation, it was off to lunch with the agency head, then on to his country club for a friendly competitive round of golf with Griswald Gravure, Dedmete's biggest customer.

It was past 5:00 P.M. when Jones and Gravure headed into the clubhouse. Jones decided to go home rather than back to the office, but first he called in for messages. His secretary read off the list of calls received—only one seemed unusual, from a Mr. Felix Nyfenbach of Piranha Industries, a British concern, requesting him to call back as soon as possible.

Jones thought it over and, as Nyfenbach had called from London and it was already 11:00 P.M. there, he decided to wait until Monday. He then drove home, content and at peace with himself—especially since he had cured his hook on the back nine.

On Sunday, Jones accompanied his family to church. At about the time the sermon began, the automatic facsimile machine in his office began churning and beeping, but its output would remain unread until the following Monday morning. By then, the snowball would be already rolling fast.

As soon as Jones walked in the door, his executive vice president handed him the fax. It was a letter, which read:

"Dear Mr. Jones:

"We apologize for transmitting this letter by facsimile machine, but we were unable to reach you by telephone.

"Pursuant to Section 803.5(a)(1) of the Rules of the United States Federal Trade Commission under Section 7A of the Clayton Act as added by Title II of the Hart-Scott-Rodino Antitrust Improvements Act of 1976 (the 'Act'), you are hereby notified as follows:

"The acquiring person is Piranha Industries and the entities controlled by it (collectively 'Piranha').

"Piranha intends to acquire voting securities of Dedmete Industries.

"Piranha intends to acquire up to all of the outstanding shares of Dedmete common stock, $1.00 par value, through open-market purchases, privately negotiated transactions, or otherwise and is filing under the Act to exceed the 50 percent threshold. . . . "

The letter went on a bit and was signed "Yours, truly mine," by Nyfenbach. The corporate treasurer ran in—

Dedmete stock was up six points, and the nightmare had begun. . . .

* * *

The corporate landscape has been changed by hostile takeovers the way the map of Europe was changed by World War I. Some large corporations have grown much larger; others have disappeared entirely.

There has been considerable discussion as to whether the hostile takeover has been a productive enterprise. Proponents contend that weak, inefficient, entrenched managements are dislodged and replaced by more competent executives in the wake of a takeover, to the benefit of shareholders and American business in general. Critics counter that more and more it is the well-run, profitable company that has become the target of corporate raiders, who want to get their hands on the company's most valuable assets—its "crown jewels." They care not a whit about the people whose jobs are eliminated when less profitable operations are sold off or shut down.

As we have seen in recent years, break-up value has supplanted book value as the criterion for determining attractive targets, and those firms with the good fortune to be unfettered by a large amount of debt, and in possession of significant cash holdings, are at grave potential risk.

If your company is private or closely held, you may think hostile takeovers are not your problem. But, what if your biggest customer or supplier is publicly held? If either were taken over, your business could be adversely affected, to say the least. Still, there is little you can do to prevent it from happening. (You can, of course, have alternate suppliers lined up—big customers are another matter.)

On the other hand, if yours is a publicly traded corporation, there is always the risk that someone will come along who decides that he or she can run your business better than you can—or at least make better use of your company's assets. And things happen pretty fast after that.

Many learned commentators have opined about the course of forced mergers over the years. It is certainly not a new phenomenon. Back in the early days of the twentieth century, some of the greatest American companies were put together under conditions of financial pressure. Alfred Sloan strung together several small car companies and formed General Motors. The fabled J. Pierpont Morgan similarly stitched together some small steel companies into the great US Steel.

After World War II, there was a movement toward conglomeratization, which we noted earlier. Some of that piling together of companies was done under duress. The hostile takeover was introduced by some conglomerators who couldn't bring the marriages about in reasonably amorous fashion. Mostly those aggressive financiers were viewed as a new strain of robber barons, harking back to the kind of characters Ida Tarbell wrote about. People like James Ling and Charles Bluhdorn who put together giant companies, often using hostile techniques, were considered to be "outsiders" in the clubby business world. The hostile takeover was generally frowned upon as a device employed by so-called corporate raiders.

Then in the early seventies, the International Nickel Company of Canada (INCO), a very establishment company, launched a hostile takeover effort against ESB Battery Company. The campaign was orchestrated by Morgan Stanley, one of the most prestigious and "in" of all investment banking firms. The American business world was startled, but quickly reassessed the picture. Hostile takeovers became known as "aggressive acquisition efforts," and gradually some of the most establishment companies in the United States (such as General Electric, Mobil Oil, and Philip Morris) got into the game. Virtually all the top investment banks got into the action, and now many of the biggest commercial banks (Morgan Guaranty, Bankers Trust) are pushing hard to be major players as well.

Recently Europe and Asia also have begun showing an appetite for the takeover game. Many European companies see bargains galore in the United States at the same time that they fear becoming targets themselves if they don't get bigger faster.

A combination of deregulation of their securities markets and the European Community's plans to remove existing trade barriers by 1992 has increased the incentive of European business managers.

First of all, they see in the United States the bushels of companies that have been selling at bargain levels since the October 1987 crash. Secondly, many of them are flush with strong currency cash and they are looking at U.S. companies evaluated in weak dollars.

And finally, there is the matter of favorable accounting

rules. In the United States, "good-will," those intangibles that are not backed up by hard assets but which make a purchase more strategically valuable, (brand names, for example), have to be written off. In Europe they can become a legitimate part of the purchase price. Thus an American company is at a disadvantage when it competes with a European company for another company. The American company is buying less "value" and therefore getting less for its dollar than the European company gets for its mark or franc.

With all these advantages and motivations, it is small wonder that we have seen a quickening invasion from across the Atlantic. Only concern about the reaction to this cultural shock in the U.S. Congress has slowed the equivalent onslaught from across the Pacific. But highly motivated lobbyists are working hard to neutralize that situation, too.

Meanwhile let's take a look at some of these foreign aggrandizers and their approach to the American industrial scene.

The British are the veterans of the foreign takeover game in the United States. They have less of a culture problem vis-à-vis Americans than most of the other foreign financial interests. They see many American companies in terms of the sum of the parts being actually greater than the stated value of the whole. Like new car strippers on the streets of New York or Chicago, the British see, a $10,000 new car as worth $50,000 in parts. Many of the British are acting like the American takeover specialists of the previous decade.

Leading the charge are the blue-blooded Sir James Gold-smith, Lord Hanson, and Sir Gordon White, with the Saatchi Brothers doing their number in the advertising and consulting businesses.

The Canadians have been very active, too. Mr. Campeau's victory in the Federated Stores sweepstakes, after having overpowered Allied Stores, makes him clearly Canada's number 1 raider. The Reichmann family has also been quite active, although they almost never seem to win. Nevertheless, they walk away with pots of money, to play again another day.

The Swiss, as of this writing, have begun to show an unusual appetite for hostility. Hoffman-LaRoche kicked it off with a surprisingly rich offer for Sterling Drug, which they increased three times before being thwarted by an even bigger figure from Eastman Kodak. Now there are rumors of several other efforts being confected in the Alps.

The Italian champion Carlo de Benedetti caused a furor in Europe in early 1988 by charging after the ponderous Société General de Belgique. He showed that Europeans can attack Europeans as well as Americans. Then Pirelli made a hostile offer for the giant Firestone Tire Company, which at the time was in the process of selling a portion of itself to Japan's Bridgestone Tire. The Pirelli offer prompted an immense counteroffer by Bridgestone for *all* of Firestone, which they subsequently won. Weeks later, the pride-wounded Pirelli settled for a consolation prize: the old Armstrong Tire Company, now called Armtek.

The French, to this point, have not been very active on the

hostile front but seem to be hoarding their cash. Their Thomson Company did do a friendly takeover of GE Consumer Electronics—a sort of barter deal—whereby they exchanged some of their own medical electronics divisions.

The Japanese, sitting with perhaps the greatest pile of capital in the world, have moved very carefully in the United States. Perhaps this is because they feel they have the greatest cultural problem of all. It is only 40 years since "Remember Pearl Harbor" was sung out in every town in America.

But one maverick Japanese company, Dainippon, did carry out the first Japanese hostile takeover of an American company in late 1987 when Reichhold Chemical succumbed to them. Recently, as noted, there has been the Firestone takeover, which wouldn't have happened except for the intrusion of Pirelli, and also the $2 billion acquisition of the CBS Records division by Sony. Furthermore, there is reported to be a lot of Japanese money going into minority partnership positions with major American investment banks and into big equity acquisition funds.

Even a small country like Denmark has gotten into the merger game. Northern Feather, a Danish down specialist, made a surprise friendly offer in early 1988 for Chatham Manufacturing, a small old-time textile company in North Carolina. Having no white knight prepared to come to its rescue, Chatham succumbed peacefully.

Whether the threat to your company comes from abroad or from within the United States, the specific hostile takeover can wreak havoc on your company. However, this is one form of battle wherein the public relations pen can be as mighty as the legal/financial sword.

We note, of course, that your company might not be the target—*you* may be seeking to acquire another company. In this case, too, communications can make a significant difference in the success or failure of the attempt and certainly is crucial to the successful integration of one company into another after the votes are counted and the money changes hands.

Let's look for a moment at the latter instance. If you are trying to acquire a company that does not wish to be acquired, remember that the target usually has the advantage of at least beginning with public sympathy on its side. The major thrust of the target's communications will be the contention that (1) it has a long record of building shareholder value, and (2) your sole interest in acquiring the company is to break it up and sell off the pieces.

Your job, then, at least from a communications standpoint, would be to counter these statements by demonstrating that shareholders have not been well served by the company's management. For example, you might point out that money invested in the target company would have grown at a faster rate in T-bills. Furthermore, you must be prepared to document why your acquisition of the target company will actually benefit shareholders, employees, and the local community. Point to your long track record of earnings growth, of enhanced shareholder value, and smart management. If you have acquired other companies in the past, note how well they are doing today, how everyone has benefited from your infusion of capital and management talent.

Finally, the best way to prove that you wish to enhance shareholder value is by means of a generous tender offer. If it is generous enough, it may actually be "preemptive," and your struggle may end very quickly. But, one always tries not to overpay for anything, and a figure short of "preemptive" leaves you open to claims by the target management that your offer is insufficient. You'll have to convince the shareholders and the securities analysts that your offer is fair.

Once you have announced your intentions, generally by means of filing a 13-D disclosure form with the SEC (mandatory once you cross the 5-percent-of-outstanding-stock threshold), you can expect the price of the target's shares to skyrocket. If the price holds firm at or slightly below the price you have offered, then the Street thinks it's a fair offer. Assuming you can line up the financing for the deal, you should be able to move along quite smartly. If, however, the share price achieves a level somewhat over the price you have offered, then the Street thinks your offer is low and that either you will have to make a sweetened offer or that some other bidder will.

Assume that the offer looks good. You now have to convince shareholders that they should tender their shares to you. If a significant portion of the stock is held by institutions and arbitrageurs, you shouldn't have too much trouble convincing them to sell. Individual stockholders, however, may pose a different problem, as they very often have come by the stock for emotional reasons (such as, they work for the company in question). And many small stockholders have an affliction known as inertia.

You can communicate with the target company's share-holders and employees through direct letters and advertisements in local papers as well as the *Wall Street Journal*. If the target company has been foolish enough to publicly reject your offer without engaging in "due diligence," you can use that rejection as proof that the target's management is entrenched and its members are concerned only about protecting their jobs. You can also document all of the slipshod management practices you believe have caused the company to be in the uninspiring condition it is. (Actually, these letters and ads often bear a remarkable resemblance to the Declaration of Independence, with its point-by-point citing of the abuses of King George.)

These communications are also the hallmark of the newly resurgent proxy contest, in which the aggressor tries to line up enough shareholder support to get himself or herself a few well-chosen friends elected to the board of directors.

Winning a proxy contest is like winning a political election race. It helps to buy a lot of votes (called "shares" in the business world), but you have to win a majority of all the votes to get your slate of directors in. (Unless there is a by-law provision for cumulative voting, in which case votes can be massed against a few of the management-supported directors.)

So you have to convince shareholders that they stand a better chance of getting a bigger return on their investment with your board nominees in place. In the case of a provision for staggered board elections, the aggressor can at least put a strong dissident faction in place on the board, rendering it incapable of getting anything meaningful done. As a result, hopefully, it will cave in to the aggressor's demands.

With junk bonds falling out of favor, proxy fights may be staging a comeback because they can be significantly cheaper to win. In general, though, the tender offer is the preferred means of swallowing up a fellow fish, if you can raise the money. It is certainly the best option open to foreign aggressors.

Once your intention to make a tender offer is public knowledge, you should also go to great pains to meet with local legislators, who will be concerned about employment and tax revenues. Be prepared to show how your ownership of the company will stimulate growth in the region, increase employment, and improve the quality of life of the area in general. The best you can usually hope for is that these local legislators will sit on the sidelines. But once in a great blue moon, a maverick politician will actually come out in favor of the acquisition because it could bring new creativity to the region.

After that, for all intents and purposes, it's a waiting game—waiting to see who tenders and who doesn't—but if you have done your homework and your offer represents a fair premium and a sound strategy, the odds shift to your team.

If you are successful, your work has just begun. Your new employees must be made to feel secure or else morale, already low since you won, will plummet further. The conquered senior management will know its days are numbered, and so their productivity is nonexistent. It is very important, however, to keep as many as possible of the good second-echelon executives from jumping ship.

One of the new stars of the leveraged buy out is Reginald Lewis, who bought Beatrice International Foods. One tactic Lewis employs to smooth the way for the takeover is to offer a percentage of the company's stock to the managers he wants to retain. There is no better way to encourage loyalty and initiative than to give key managers a piece of the action.

You will need to establish your own ties to the community. Essentially, this means beginning to manage your impact among all audiences, paying particular attention to the ones who potentially can do you the most harm—legislators, union leaders, and most importantly, the middle managers you need to keep on board to keep the company running.

For the public relations professional, often the most testing action is on the defensive side. Helping your company defend itself from a hostile takeover demands creativity, high energy, and a certain ruthlessness—the same qualities you'll see in lawyers and investment bankers who specialize in such matters.

In our little anecdote about Sam Jones earlier in this section, we noted that the letter represented the beginning of the nightmare. The hostile takeover attempt is perhaps the most feared event in corporate management circles. When it finally ends, the takeover attempt, whether successful or not, will have radically changed your company. Your life and those of your employees will never be the same.

At the first hint that a takeover attempt might be brewing, you should immediately line up legal, financial, and communications counsel. Actually, many companies, realizing that a takeover attempt could develop seemingly overnight, establish relationships with these counselors well in advance of anything actually happening. A few large law firms that specialize in mergers and acquisitions have many clients who pay monthly retainers just to ensure that no other company can hire these experts to go after them.

Legal and financial experts will ultimately provide you with the ammunition (in the form of a restructuring or a counteroffer from a friendly suitor or "white knight"), but there are several communications initiatives you can undertake to contribute to the fight.

Hold the strategy you would use in acquiring a company up to a mirror, and in many ways your path is clear. You need to convince your target audiences that the company is better off under your management than it would be under that of the aggressor. Here is where managing your corporate impact as an ongoing strategy really pays off.

Your first concern has to be the shareholders. If a significant block of your stock is held by institutions, pay them a personal visit and remind them of the steps you have taken in the past to enhance shareholder value. Explain what steps you will be taking to further enhance it. Ask for their support when the tender offer is made.

Understand that they will be sympathetic to a point but that their primary responsibility is as a fiduciary for the funds they manage. They have to do whatever is in the best interest of their own stakeholders.

Legislators are another important potential source of support, but in the face of a takeover attempt, it's too late to make a campaign contribution. However, even if you haven't been going out of your way to massage politicians, they may still be interested in hearing how the hostile acquisition could put thousands of their voters out of work and significantly trim tax revenues.

Also, there has been enough history following the earlier hostile takeovers to show that they often work out to no one's benefit except a handful of speculators. Meanwhile, communities have been thrown into turmoil. As a result, more and more states are enacting legislation to impede hostile takeovers. Sometimes these measures can be overcome in court, but litigation takes time, and time is on the side of the target.

Another tactic is to try to show that the company will not be successful under the proposed new management. When Harcourt Brace Jovanovich successfully repelled avowed Socialist Robert Maxwell and British Printing and Communications Corporation (primarily through a massive restructuring that made the erstwhile attractive company highly unattractive overnight), one of the communications tactics undertaken was to suggest (and back up with testimonials) that state education commissioners would not buy textbooks from a Socialist publisher. This development could have cost the company as much as one third—$400 million—of its annual income. The objective was to give second thoughts to Maxwell's financiers in Europe.

This ploy doesn't always work. When Martin Sorrell's WPP Group made a tender offer for JWT Group, the holding company that owned the J. Walter Thompson advertising agency, JWT convinced one of its largest and most tenured clients, Goodyear, to threaten to leave if the acquisition took place. The threat was completely ignored by Wall Street, and even after the acquisition was consummated, and Goodyear did, indeed, take its business elsewhere, most analysts took it in stride.

What JWT failed to consider was this: Analysts had assumed that JWT would lose more clients on its own due to sloppy management and loss of talent than through the acquisition. One of Sorrell's first moves after the acquisition was to entice certain former Thompson executives to return to the company, a move which pleased clients more than the acquisition displeased them.

JWT also banked on clients really caring whether the agency was acquired. Agency watchers had always assumed that a hostile takeover of an agency could not be successful because the top creative people would leave. JWT didn't take into account that the agency was already hemorrhaging talent—almost any development that stemmed that flow would be welcomed by clients and employees alike, and a takeover that uprooted the current management might work as well as anything else.

Since the successful defense of a takeover attempt may well mean encumbering your company with substantial debt, some capital or R&D expenditures will have to be put on hold. Planned expansions will go to the back burner, and a hiring freeze—if not layoffs—will commence. You may have to sell off divisions of the company to raise cash and, in doing so, incur the wrath of employees and other audiences as much as if you were the aggressor. Nothing is particularly fair in this game.

In each step of this process, communications has a crucial

role. Whether it is a matter of convincing the financial community that your company will continue to be viable in the face of the substantial new debt incurred or reassuring stockholders that you have acted in their best interests in aggressively defending the company from the attack, your communications function will be put to the test.

Generally speaking, all stops are pulled in such efforts. Cost becomes almost irrelevant as, in the words of one embattled executive we knew, "If we win, it will be worth whatever it costs. If we lose, no one will give a damn anymore."

* * *

As soon as Sam Jones got to his desk, he called Chute, Furst, & Wynn, the big-time New York law firm that specialized in mergers and acquisitions. Jones had retained the firm months ago just in case Dedmete became a target. Perry Chute, the senior partner, had seen the activity in Dedmete stock and had already booked a flight. He suggested that Jones call in Dedmete's investment banker, Roland N. Dough & Co.

Banker conferred with lawyer and issued joint instructions to Jones: Do nothing until you hear from us. Don't stray too far from the phone, but don't answer it if it rings, either.

By noon, the hired guns began arriving on the scene. Perry Chute and his entourage of 12 associates set up in the conference room. With them were six partners from their Big Eight accounting firm. The accounting firm was expecting four partners from its law firm. Sixteen investment bankers were ensconced in the accounting department. In addition, the bankers brought a total of nine representatives from their law and accounting firms.

An account executive from Dedmete's public relations firm, Wright, Place, & Bill, sat on the sofa in Jones's office.

At 6:30 P.M., Jones was summoned into a meeting with the assembled troops. After 15 minutes, he emerged with a long list written on a legal pad. His staff gathered around, awaiting his bidding.

"Okay," said Jones. "We need two orders of Moo Goo Gai Pan, three pastrami on rye with mustard. One tuna on a roll, no mayo . . . ." He reeled off the dinner order. His staff split up and headed off for the various restaurants in town.

For three days, the lawyers and bankers talked among themselves, consuming enormous quantities of take-out food. (Jones, with little else to do, calculated that the assemblage had disposed of more than 937 eggrolls alone.) Finally, at 3:30 P.M. on the fourth day, they summoned Jones again. Jones, unshaven and still wearing the suit he had worn three days earlier, was instructed that he had reviewed the offer from Nyfenbach and rejected it as insufficient. (This came as a considerable surprise to Jones, since he had yet to see a copy of the Piranha filing.) A press release was prepared, and an envoy was sent to Washington to file the requisite documents with the SEC. The first bills from the consultants arrived, each well into six figures.

The lawyers and bankers ensconced themselves for three more days. Jones helped with the dishes.

At last he was summoned to another meeting, at which he was told that the problem had been solved. Roland N. Dough would advance Dedmete just over $300 million in a huge leveraged recapitalization. Shareholders would receive a one-time $33 dividend. The company would have to sell off its specialty chemical division, but the packaging division would remain. Roland N. Dough would take a 44 percent ownership position in the company. It was projected that through massive cost-cutting and increased prices, Dedmete would be able to pay off its stupendous debt within five years.

Roland N. Dough, by the way, would have three seats on the eight-person board of directors.

Not surprisingly, as soon as the deal was announced publicly, Nyfenbach announced he was no longer interested in Dedmete. In a Reuters interview, he compared the deal to giving all of one's food to one's cat so that the mice would starve.

The lawyers and bankers shook Jones's hand and slapped him on the back. "Congratulations," they said. "You've stayed independent. What a brilliant plan you came up with!"

Jones excused himself to finish sorting the silverware and have a good cry.

9

Getting More Clients

The Fine Art of Self-Promotion

Chapter 9

Overheard on a commuter train in Westchester County:

"What do you think about lawyers advertising?"

"Oh, it's the hot thing now. All the old barriers are breaking down; all the professions are doing it. It was ridiculous for the ABA to be against it for so long. Lawyers are in business, just like their clients, and competition is stiffer than ever."

"So, your firm is advertising?"

"Of course not. Nobody who's any good does that."

Contrary to what even they have maintained, lawyers and accountants have aggressively marketed their services for years. They may have referred to their activities as "practice development," but it boils down to the same thing: getting more clients.

Participation in seminars, authoring books and articles, making speeches, being quoted in news stories about issues and trends—all of these time-honored public relations activities help to create awareness of a professional and his or her firm.

But actually referring to these efforts as public relations—that's where professionals (and the professional societies to which they belong) traditionally drew the line until the mid-seventies, when ethical restrictions were relaxed.

As noted by the anecdote, the relaxing of taboos did not lead to universal acceptance. However, lawyers, accountants, and even doctors are being drawn into traditional marketing in ever growing numbers.

Marketing professional services is different from marketing soap or cars. Generally speaking, what is really being marketed are the experience and talents of a few people. Since such attributes are not often self-evident from a picture, one needs a means of demonstrating them.

In most businesses and professions, there are one or two "industry leaders" who seem to be quoted more than anyone else. While these individuals may be among the best in the business, there are others who can speak with equal authority, given the chance. What these oft-quoted experts have is inclination and time.

If you, too, have the inclination and the time, the first hurdle is to overcome the resistance within the firm to aggressive promotion. Get past that, and the rest will be a cakewalk.

ACCOUNTANTS

Let's look at accountants first—for a good reason. While the principles discussed in this section apply to virtually any profession, no profession provides better opportunities for promotion than accounting. Yet, after several years of freedom to self-promote, there is still no single entity or person who speaks for the accounting profession. Not even the chairman of the American Institute of Certified Public Accountants (AICPA) does so. Many firms' partners are quoted in specific stories about taxes or pension accounting, but for accounting profession issues, no one speaks as the expert. The profession is currently faced with unprecedented challenges to its ethics and contribution to society. This is no time to keep a low profile.

As one of many examples, a front-page article in the June 23, 1987 issue of the *Wall Street Journal* discussed opinion shopping and the SEC's call for increased disclosure. The story mentioned several companies who would object to the plan, but despite the fact that accounting firms would be at the vortex of the issue, not one was quoted, or even cited.

This is not a new phenomenon. Commenting on substantive issues has generally gone against the grain of accounting firm partners. Many are distrustful of the press; others are fearful of alienating their peers or clients. Yet the seriousness of the issues facing the profession demands that it respond effectively.

Where there is a need, opportunity lies. Aside from the benefits derived from having a spokesperson to publicly defend the interests of the profession, one must consider the business benefits that assumption of the leader/spokesperson role offers. Although no national figure has assumed the leadership role, there is nothing to stop you from becoming a regional expert.

Clients of any profession enjoy confirmation that they made a smart choice in selecting your firm, and they take comfort in knowing that anyone examining that choice will find no fault. They also like to know that their accounting firm is at the forefront of the profession. What better way is there to reinforce that perception than by means of the "third-party" credibility one gains from being quoted regularly in the business press?

Not to belabor the obvious, becoming the recognized leader requires leadership. As is the case with corporate visibility, professional communications requires taking a leadership stance on the issues facing the profession and the general business community. It also requires taking a risk.

The main risk is that the spokesperson will express an opinion on a given issue, only to be proven in hindsight to have been off base. Nobody enjoys this, of course, but plenty of people (economists come to mind immediately) who are willing to take that risk occasionally get clobbered. Yet they continue to enjoy the respect and ear of the business community.

With the movement toward becoming global, "one-stop-shopping" consultancies, accounting firms have crossed the Rubicon. More and more firms have expanded their menu of services to include such nontraditional disciplines as marketing and computer systems analysis. Suddenly, their competition is not just other accounting firms but also such conglomerates as Saatchi and Saatchi, which has stated its goal as becoming the only business consultant anyone will ever need. However, accounting firms of all sizes have, for the moment, a leg up on other business consultants—they possess an intimate knowledge of how businesses of all types work, domestically and abroad.

Accountants are as qualified as any other professionals, if not more so, to comment on business and economic trends, but they virtually never do. Part of the reason has to do with the residual uneasiness many firms still feel about self-promotion.

The bracing breeze of competition has demanded new approaches to marketing, but many partners remain uncomfortable with the idea of actively marketing themselves vis-à-vis their competitors. The fact that most major firms have embarked on ambitious marketing efforts doesn't necessarily mean that they *enjoy* press attention—on the contrary, they would prefer it if their competitors would simply stop getting so much of it. It's a matter of keeping up with the Andersens. In reality, though, most of this publicity is related to specific developments in accounting, such as the new tax laws, and rarely deals with the larger issues facing the profession.

Also, as noted, there is a hesitation to speak out on issues because of a fear of alienating clients as well as fellow partners. This hesitation led one reporter from a major business publication, who had been invited to interview several partners of a Big Eight firm in an attempt to dispel the firm's stodgy reputation, to conclude that the reputation was well earned.

There can be no half steps on the path to increased visibility. Messages need to be developed and incorporated into a cohesive communications strategy. That strategy must then be implemented. Audiences should be identified and messages delivered in a clear, understandable fashion—preferably taking one side or another of a specific issue in no uncertain terms. Thus, there needs to be a consensus to overcome the fear of toe-stepping. To that end, consider using focus groups or roundtable luncheons composed of professional staff drawn from throughout the firm. The objective is to determine and discuss issues on which the firm can take a stand, with the goal of developing a uniform and clearly stated position.

A quick look at the challenges facing the accounting profession yields several possibilities—possibilities that can be exploited on a national, regional, or local level. Recent congressional hearings have raised issues that go right to the heart of the profession. How do you deter fraud? How far does the auditor's responsibility extend when it comes to determining fraud? Do accounting firms give in too easily to client pressure to "bend the rules" in their favor? Can a firm perform an objective audit with the left hand while earning big fees for providing business counsel with the right? Is the profession capable of implementing reforms itself, or is there a need for greater government regulation? In a day and age when continuous financial disclosure may become the norm, how do you carry out adequate evaluation and reporting of internal controls?

As the same time, to be perceived as a business leader, a firm needs to address the larger issues that affect us all. Should Congress repeal the Glass-Steagall Act? Should the United States retaliate against countries that run up large trade surpluses or are guilty of dumping? What are this country's options when it comes to cutting the budget deficit, and which one is most desirable? Is there too much greed on Wall Street? Are our children growing up with the right kind of values? What is the economic agenda for America in the twenty-first century?

Tough questions all, with no easy answers. But in seeking the answers, a firm can define the kind of company it is. It will also display, before all the world, corporate courage, insight, and leadership.

Once the issues and the firm's official policy toward them have been determined, finding opportunities to express your positions should present little difficulty. Reporters are always on the lookout for new sources for comment, and accounting firms are blessed with an enviable credibility among business leaders and the general public— certainly when compared to the esteem in which other professionals are held. An AICPA-sponsored Harris Poll, ranking accountants at or near the top of most categories of public trust, made that clear.

ATTORNEYS

As is the case in other professions, the principle of client loyalty has been sorely tested of late. Long-time clients are shopping around, looking at counsel on a transactional basis, seeking out specialists for each case.

Meanwhile, many companies are increasing their internal legal staffs, taking business away from the law firms. Clients are asking for more and more detailed explanations of activities, prying into the inner workings of the law firm, forcing much self-examination.

New business from old sources is drying up, but the need for firms to grow—to attract and hold bright new associates and to keep up with increased financial pressures—is growing itself.

Many firms' top partners are having to turn more and more of their attention to the uncomfortable chore of business-getting. "Selling!" they say with disgust. "Hey, we came into this business to be lawyers, not salespeople!"

Well, those days are over. Law firms are faced with many of the same challenges as their brethren in accounting, medicine, and, for that matter, public relations.

To get new business and hang onto existing clients, you have to be a winner. That means you have to look and act like one. You have to have a certain level of visibility within the community, where you should be seen both as a forward-thinking outfit and one that is mindful of tradition.

You have to compete with other law firms not just for clients, but for the best associates. Then you have to keep those associates in a time when even seasoned partners are being lured away.

Lawyers will face the same resistance to promotional efforts among their partners as accountants; consider gaining some general agreement on such issues as:

- Why should the Delaware antitakeover statute be overturned?
- What should companies know about recent developments in age-discrimination law?

Whatever your specialty—"Ten Tips on Getting Custody of Your Child"—the local paper would probably love to hear from you, especially if you can write (or have written) an article that puts legal theory into layman's terms.

As for attracting bright associates, take a look at the materials you have published about your firm for recruitment use (if any): Do they portray your business as an exciting, "cutting-edge" organization or an old line, white shoe, family retainer kind of firm? Do a little research. Find out what the type of associate you're looking for is seeking in an employer and try to reflect those qualities.

PHYSICIANS

One of the great myths about the medical profession is that its members do not self-promote. If that were true, most of the morning news shows would have an extra 10 minutes a day to fill, at a minimum.

Using physicians as experts is time-honored. We'll never forget the sight of Dr. Art Ulene's "Today Show" photographs depicting the gruesome results of hair implant surgery gone awry. Cornflakes will never taste the same.

Whenever there is a major breakthrough in medicine, there is controversy. Where there is controversy, there is a need for an expert to be quoted on one side or the other. Why not you?

Write a short bylined article for the local paper: "Why a second opinion can save your life."

Does it work? When *New York Magazine* did a cover story on the latest cosmetic fad in the Big Apple, tooth bonding (a process that has been compared to retiling one's bathroom), the article quoted most of the handful of dentists in New York who know how to do the procedure. Shortly after publication, getting an appointment to have one's teeth bonded was more difficult than getting an audience with the Pope.

GENERAL TACTICS FOR PROFESSIONALS

The designated spokesperson, presumably the managing partner or chairman—or hospital chief of staff, for example—should pursue opportunities to meet with reporters to discuss topical issues. An effort should also be made to contact business, law, or medical reporters whenever a "breaking" story develops about which the spokesperson can render an informed opinion. One can't wait for reporters to call. They work under tight deadlines and are inclined to look to past reliable sources for quotable material and reactions in a hurry.

Also, the spokesperson should get to know the reporters who follow the profession. In smaller cities it may be a general business reporter. Larger cities have a "beat" reporter. Periodic meetings with reporters "for background" can be mutually beneficial. The goal is to have the spokesperson's name added to the reporter's Rolodex (major newspapers have computerized files of quotable sources, accessible to all reporters) and over a relatively short period of time several reporters may call, on a variety of topics.

Another effective tactic is to write an Op-Ed article on a timely topic (it can be "ghost-written"). Physicians should try not to sound as if they are writing for the *New England Journal of Medicine* unless they seek other doctors as patients. Particularly in the case of lawyers and accountants, such articles, once published, can be reprinted (with the publication's permission, of course) and sent to clients and prospects. The reprint should be circulated internally, too, to remind partners and staff that they are part of a dynamic firm.

Media relations is but one way to heighten visibility. Speeches allow one to target a message to a specific group. Seek out opportunities to speak before any credible audience—business clubs, industry forums, and in smaller cities, even Rotary Clubs. Prospects and clients can be invited to attend, which can lead to new business and bolster existing client confidence.

And . . . say something interesting. Nothing is more frustrating than listening to 40 minutes of "on the other hand" and "then again. . . ." The listeners may not always agree with the speech, but they should be impressed with the speaker's sincerity, courage, and logic. After the speech is given, the text should be sent to newspapers and trade publications, with a short, covering press release that summarizes the main points.

These tactics will work at any level—Big Eight firms for *Business Week* or Sam Jones, CPA (J.D. or M.D.) on a local or regional level. A reporter in Syracuse would rather quote a local source than one from Philadelphia, and since most of your clients will be drawn from your region, it makes sense to put the bulk of your effort into local promotion.

10

Visibility Challenges

The Environment,
Product Tampering, AIDS,
Corporate Crime

ENVIRONMENTAL CONCERNS

If there is one area on which communications counselors agree, it is the growth of environmental issues as a communications challenge, now and for the future. Every day, it seems, the media relate the unsettling details of another environmental insult that corporate America has perpetrated on an unsuspecting and defenseless public. Not even companies that assiduously manage their corporate impact are immune from criticism, and you have to be prepared to respond effectively whether your company is "guilty" or not.

Even if a crisis itself cannot be managed, you can manage your response to it—and manage it you must, or you can just as easily compound the problem. Because an environmental crisis can take years to resolve, dealing with it can become virtually a second career for the embattled executive.

The number of environmental crises reported has been on the rise in recent years, which seems strange on the surface. We know, for example, that we are not getting *less* careful in the handling and disposal of toxic materials. As a matter of fact, much of the contamination being discovered today was introduced to the environment years ago. Indeed, part of the problem is that once introduced, contaminants can remain in the soil, water, or air almost indefinitely. Why are we seeing so many more revelations about contamination of natural resources today than in decades past? There are several reasons:

- We are, as a society, more sensitive to environmental issues than ever before.

- We are more cognizant of the carcinogenic dangers of certain chemicals than ever before.
- Finally, the technology for detecting hazardous levels of chemicals in water, for example, has steadily improved over the years, making large gains in sensitivity and reliability in the last five to ten years.

With regard to the first two points, consumer consciousness may represent an even greater challenge than regulators' zeal, thanks to the passage of SARA Title III, the so-called Community Right To Know (CRTK) Act. CRTK is an outgrowth of the demands of citizen activist groups to know what potentially hazardous substances are being used in their communities. That in itself doesn't seem an unreasonable demand. CRTK, however, may be an unreasonable response. Be that as it may, you will still have to deal with what could become one of your greatest challenges in managing your corporate impact.

CRTK stipulates that community boards—called Local Emergency Planning Committees (LEPCs)—must be provided with complete data regarding the substances used and emissions produced at facilities within their purview. The data the committees are entitled to include "raw" figures, with no explanations, and to the uninitiated, can be quite disconcerting (for example, with no accompanying explanation, data may reveal that your facility emits "millions of pounds" of some substance each year). A reporter who smells a story could make considerable hay out of that statistic, never bothering to mention that the substance is nontoxic and occurs in nature in far greater quantities. Better yet, you might be shown on camera saying as much—while the reporter, in essence, says "Oh, sure, that's what we'd expect you to say." Good for TV news ratings. Bad for business.

CRTK is particularly noteworthy because it empowers the LEPCs only to extract and disseminate information—not to enforce laws or in any way enjoin a company from doing what it always has done. The idea, though, is that public pressure is an even more potent force than the law and that communities, aroused by the knowledge that potentially hazardous materials are in use in their midst, will apply the necessary pressure to make a company "clean up its act." In effect, you are on the receiving end of the "public impact," and you can manage it just like your corporate impact and with the same weapon: information.

If you have maintained good relations with the local community, you can work with the LEPCs to examine the raw data in perspective. You can provide additional backup data to explain just what certain chemicals do and how they can affect those who come in contact with them. Note, too, how many of these chemicals are found in nature and in common household products. You can also document your safety procedures and the unlikeliness of an accident.

Most of all, you can do your best to appear as cooperative and candid as possible—it is your only defense against community activists who want to portray you as a venal, "stonewalling" corporation.

CRTK is especially vexing because it has the potential to get your company in trouble for doing nothing wrong at all. But don't let aggravation over CRTK allow you to decrease your vigilance with regard to presenting real cases of environmental contamination. In the long run, these events continue to have far greater implications for your company than CRTK because, unlike the LEPCs, your opponents in these matters—for example, the Environmental Protection Agency (EPA)—have real teeth and an insatiable hunger for corporate hide.

Authorities such as the EPA have strict criteria as to what constitutes a "safe" level of abnormal chemicals in drinking water. For instance, in the case of certain organic chemicals, two parts per billion is considered the maximum allowable concentration based on the presumed health effects of a daily consumption of two liters of water contaminated with a given chemical over a period of 70 years. The "safe enough" level is the amount of the chemical one can ingest without increasing one's risk of cancer, all other factors being equal. Not everyone accepts the efficacy of this criterion—certainly not the consumers of the tainted water, at least—and the public will not be supportive of any attempts to dismiss minute levels of contamination. Nevertheless, the supposition inherent in such criteria does give you a shadow of a foothold in your defense.

Tread carefully. Crises in general are emotional issues, but environmental crises give rise to deeper and stronger emotions than most. The loss of control over one's own health and that of one's family—the realization that one may have been consuming toxic substances for years, thereby greatly increasing the likelihood of developing one or another form of cancer—these are heartrending concerns that demand compassion, understanding, and most of all, action.

Other concerns include a negative effect on property values, slowed or arrested economic development, and even the prospect of permanent relocation away from the contaminated locale. All of these nightmares became real for the residents in the vicinity of Love Canal near Buffalo, New York, made uninhabitable by ground water contamination for which Hooker Chemical Company was held responsible. Now, whenever contamination is detected, the mind of each member of the community is flooded with the fear that they will have the same experience.

All of these factors come together to make allegations of environmental contamination one of the worst experiences you might ever face, second only to a product-tampering incident (which we will discuss later).

When confronted with the possibility that your company's manufacturing processes may have resulted in contamination of the environment, there are two crucial messages you must communicate immediately. The first is that your company is as concerned about the alleged problem as everyone else. That should be true, since you and your employees are as likely to be affected by polluted water or air as anyone else.

The second message is that you will cooperate fully with the authorities and take whatever actions are appropriate to help find a solution to the problem.

Neither of these messages conveys acceptance of the responsibility for the contamination, but they help to position you as a concerned corporate citizen.

Experience has shown that lawyers and public relations practitioners often disagree about what is and isn't "safe" to say. We naturally defer to the lawyers regarding legal matters, with this caution: Don't automatically assume that a lawyer's advice to "clam up" is entirely reasonable. It may breed even more fear and suspicion.

The next step is to analyze the allegations made by the EPA or its state counterpart (or whoever has made the allegations in question) to see if there is anything to them. Pay particular attention to determining how extensive an investigation was undertaken prior to the filing of the complaint. That information can be an eye-opener. Due to the sheer volume of cases these agencies must investigate, there is a tendency to look for the biggest target and shoot. Unfortunately, the phrasing of many of our country's environmental laws puts the burden of proof on the accused.

You may have to undertake an investigation of your own, naturally at your expense, and this investigation should be both thorough and repeatable. Use an outside consultant with impeccable credentials and be aware that you may have to invite the plaintiff's expert in to review the data and, possibly, run his or her own tests.

If the data your investigation uncovers support the allegations, the rest of the job is straightforward enough, albeit unpleasant—begin negotiating a consent agreement if possible. Doing so puts you in the somewhat transparent position of not admitting anything without exactly getting off the hook. You will still have to contribute to cleanup costs (which can be enormous), and you will have a civil liability exposure with potentially much graver consequences for your company.

On the other hand, if your data contradict the allegations,

then you have a whole new ball game, and communications can be a major factor in what is likely to be an unpleasant battle.

It is not our intention to impugn the motives of the enforcement agencies; indeed, we believe that they perform a necessary and valuable function. Most employees of these agencies are sincere in their concern for the health and well-being of the public. Sometimes, though, one wonders if that is all that impels their zealous pursuit of those who would sully our natural resources.

It would be naive to ignore the pressure these agencies are under to *perform*. Their work is expensive, and as in all areas of government, there is an increasing demand for budget justification. How should the public measure the value of a department, bureau, or agency?

A demonstrably cleaner environment would speak for itself, but significant progress does not come overnight. Years may elapse between the initial identification of a contamination source and the cleanup of the contaminated area.

What's needed is some other means of staying in the public eye. What could be better than a splashy, finger-pointing headline that at once both stirs up great public alarm *and* puts its collective mind at ease, all the while highlighting the vigilance of the public servant? It's a natural—and because it also sells papers, such "revelations" are usually met with glee by the press.

Keep in mind that government agencies are adept at press relations. All that's needed now and then is a pigeon, a name to plug into the blank space in the headline. If you're the pigeon they go after, your only hope is to bell the cat.

The post-Watergate media, reflecting the general public, are consistent in their skepticism toward government and business alike. While a headline lambasting a company for alleged pollution is attractive, most reporters are willing to at least consider the possibility that the allegations are incorrect. If your data significantly contradict those of the accusing agency, that's worthy of press attention, too.

The problem you may face, however, is that reporters are generally not scientists. Your contradictory data will probably be highly technical and too complex in their raw state for reporters to digest for readers. You must do that job for them.

From the pages and volumes of data at hand, two or three facts that clearly summarize your case must be culled. For example:

- The contamination discovered on the plant site may also appear in equal or greater concentrations half a mile away, or throughout the town, making it difficult to identify a single source.
- The chemicals identified in the allegations are inconsistent with the chemicals used in your processes.
- Plant records, including OSHA filings, and contracts with waste management firms show no incidences of spills or dumping.

At the very least, a significant variation between the data collected by the agency and those generated by your study should be grounds for a retest, to be performed by a mutually acceptable third party. Any resistance to this suggestion by the agency can be depicted as evidence of a rather shaky case.

As new developments in the matter emerge, you can count on receiving press inquiries. It is important to avoid appearing as if you have something to hide, so a timely response to such inquiries by a designated and informed spokesperson for the company is essential. Remember to keep answers as simple as possible and take advantage of any opportunity to repeat the major points you have developed.

At some point, unless you have made such an airtight case that the matter is dropped, you may face litigation. Numerous factors contribute to your decision as to how best to proceed. Among them, unfortunately, is the balance between the cost of litigating and the cost of a settlement. While on principle you may feel obliged to fight the issue to the end, that may not be a practical decision. It is entirely possible that the case may come down to a test of the constitutionality of the laws empowering the agency to act in the fashion it does. That's a big bucks proposition, particularly since the government is often empowered to exact treble damages if a company has the temerity to litigate and the bad luck to lose.

If you go the settlement route, you can attempt to present your company as acting as a good neighbor within the community to end the strife—in spite of the preponderance of evidence supporting your position. Mention, too, that you have an obligation to, say, stockholders, not to engage in costly litigation that would likely result in a

Pyrrhic victory. Let your attorneys advise you as to any civil exposure that might arise from a settlement. That can be just as compelling an argument against one.

By the way, know thine enemy. You can get into trouble with hazardous substances even if you never actually touch them, and it may not be the environmental agencies that get on your case. A few years ago, an insurance company (also one of the country's biggest pension fund managers) became embroiled in a messy suit involving toxic waste disposal—even though no contamination occurred.

The company invested a portion of a labor union's pension funds in the purchase of a parcel of land, which it then leased to a business—let's call it Luckless, Inc. Unfortunately, Luckless did indeed live up to its name.

Luckless Inc.'s manager folded his tents, and, to satisfy his obligations to the insurance company under the terms of his lease, he then subleased the property (with the insurance company's permission) to a company that happened to handle toxic waste. The insurance company, sensitive to environmental issues, demanded and received an assurance that the site would be used only as a stopover point in the shipment of these wastes, a truck stop for all intents and purposes. No waste would actually be disposed of on the site. The facility was inspected regularly and found to be well run and in compliance with all regulations. Better than that, the income from the sublease was actually significantly greater than from the original lease. So much the better for the insurance company and its pension fund client.

Eventually, however, the lease ran out, and with it, the sublease. Of its own accord, the waste disposal company vacated, leaving nary a trace of contamination. The EPA was satisfied that lessor, lessee, and sublessee had acted responsibly and with due caution for the environment. Thus, nearly three years later, the insurance company was stunned to receive notice of a suit brought against it. The suit was brought, not by the EPA, but by the Department of Labor (DOL), which alleged that despite the fact that the site remained as pristine as ever, the insurance company had acted imprudently in allowing the lessee to sublease the property to a toxic waste disposal company, which might have contaminated the site. The fact that there had not been an accident, that the insurance company had gone to great lengths to ensure that the subtenant complied with EPA and state regulations—these facts meant nothing. The DOL suit alleged that had there been an accident, the property's value would have plummeted, resulting in a substantial loss for the union's pension fund. It petitioned to have the insurance company buy the property from the pension fund, just to make sure that the fund would be protected from any losses in the future.

Ultimately, the insurance company did buy the property from the pension fund, and the site's value appreciated as the company expected, but the legal costs associated with the suit cut into the profits considerably—and, of course, unnecessarily.

In this instance, press coverage was heaviest in the pension-fund-management trade publications, with little exposure in the general business media—unfortunately, of course, the decision makers at major pension funds read both. The press relations objective was to stay out of the press to the extent possible. That was accomplished primarily by issuing a statement that the company's policy was not to comment on matters in litigation—perfectly reasonable, except that it does eventually present the problem of what to do once a judgment or settlement is reached. In this case, although the internal public relations staff happened to be of the highest caliber, management's decision was to decline to comment.

The public relations department, if it had been given the chance, would have tried to depict the company's actions as responsible, particularly as opposed to those of the DOL. As it was, and as one would have expected, the DOL made considerable hay out of the occasion. Handling toxic waste sure is a risky business.

While we're taking shots at government agencies, let's not forget the Food and Drug Administration.

The Cranberry Crisis

Not all environmental crises involve air or water pollution, and you don't even have to be guilty of anything to suffer at the hands of federal regulators.

Several years ago, an official of the Food and Drug Administration (FDA), acting on some preliminary test data, issued a warning that a certain pesticide, aminotriozole, had been linked to cancer. This pesticide was most often used to spray cranberries, and the FDA advised the public to avoid eating them.

Timing is everything. Had the FDA made its announcement in June, the economic impact on food retailers would have been negligible, but unfortunately the directive was issued in—you guessed it—November, days before Thanksgiving.

The vast majority of cranberries and cranberry products are sold during November and December. Although not demanded to do so by the FDA, grocery stores across the country pulled millions of cans of cranberries off the shelves. Like all the major supermarket chains, Grand Union stores were hard hit because their buyers had purchased truckloads of cranberry products in anticipation of the holiday demand. If these products were not sold by the New Year, they would languish on the shelves (or in warehouses) until the following Thanksgiving. Undoubtedly, some product would be lost due to shelf-life expiration, and just carrying that much product in inventory for so long a period was bad for business. While cranberry sales normally did not account for tremendous profits, the FDA's action made cranberries the loser of the year.

Grand Union turned to its public relations counsel for help. Could anything be done to get the berries back on the shelves in time for the holidays? As with the hypothetical example of the EPA data discussed previously, the first steps in this real-life case were to question the validity of the data produced by the FDA and to learn from the agency what they regarded as an acceptable level of aminotriozole in cranberries. An independent testing laboratory, Foster D. Snell and Co., was retained. Foster D. Snell had established his reputation through his contribution to the landmark, Reader's Digest-sponsored research into the effects of cigarette smoking. His credentials were impeccable.

Working around the clock, the Snell scientists began

sampling canned cranberries from Grand Union stores all over the country, looking for traces of aminotriozole and then measuring its concentration. What the laboratory discovered was that only cranberries from the state of Washington showed traces of the chemical in concentrations greater than had been deemed safe by the FDA. (Grand Union bought the bulk of its cranberries from the Ocean Spray cooperative in New England.)

Within a few days, self-adhesive stickers were printed bearing the message that the cranberries within had been "tested and guaranteed absolutely safe," and Grand Union employees began applying them to every cranberry can in stock. Meanwhile, the public relations firm arranged for a press conference at the largest Grand Union store in lower Manhattan. In view of television cameras and reporters from virtually every TV station and newspaper in the city—plus the bureaus of some out-of-town newspapers—the chairman of the supermarket chain ceremoniously restored to the shelf of that store the first of the tested cans of cranberries. Resulting press coverage was even better than hoped—the local New York television stations even led off their six o'clock news shows with the story. Because Grand Union stores were the only ones selling "guaranteed safe" cranberries, their shelves were soon emptied. Millions of dollars of Grand Union canned cranberries were sold in the ensuing days while other supermarkets were stuck with their inventory.

"The biggest loser of the year" became the season's hottest seller that Thanksgiving.

Incidentally, the cranberry producers' association adopted the same testing technique and managed to clear much of their product before Christmas, a month later.

PRODUCT TAMPERING

While environmental crises can be a nightmare, nothing is more gut-wrenching than a product-tampering incident. It is in such a case that the degree to which you have developed goodwill among your target audiences can actually make the difference between the survival or collapse of your company.

Although product tamperings and environmental crises share some things in common—acute anxiety on the part of both company and consumer, for example—they differ in several key respects. For one thing, the results of product tampering are immediately visible, greatly increasing the urgency of the matter. Also, tampering strikes randomly—anyone who uses the product is at risk, but like roulette, fate plays a large role. Also, unlike diseases such as cancer, in which the cause of onset is difficult to determine, the exact cause of injury or death from product tampering can be pinpointed quickly by means of a postmortem examination.

The other significant difference is that, aside from the unfortunate victims, consumers can do something to relieve their anxiety over reports of product tampering: They can stop consuming. Naturally, that action can have dire consequences for your product—consequences that may be unjustified. Your product may be the target of a one-time tampering episode or a multi-incident campaign. The difference is crucial since the latter will surely result in widespread media coverage. There's really no way to keep a lid on the story, and from a public safety standpoint, that's as it should be.

On the other hand, who is served by massive press coverage of a product tampering if it can be quickly shown to have been a one-time incident, the action of a lunatic? Certainly the public is not. Even if the tampering has been confined to an easily identifiable lot number, many consumers will think twice about using the product ever again. Maybe the next pain-relief tablet they take from the bottle in their medicine chest will be "it." There's a good chance the remaining tablets will be dumped and replaced with your competition's product, even though the consumer may have trusted and been loyal to your brand for years. Sales of your other products may be affected, too. But the most compelling reason for discretion is to minimize needless anxiety for the consumer.

A case in point: In the wake of the highly publicized Tylenol tampering case several years ago, there was a wave of similar tampering of food and over-the-counter pharmaceutical products all over the country. Most were isolated incidents with no consequent ramifications except for the public scare and damage to the products' reputations.

One such incident occurred in a Tampa, Florida, supermarket, and the actions of the public authorities and the product's manufacturer are a good example of how to avoid needless public panic and product reputation damage.

It was in the wee hours of a Sunday morning when the Richardson-Merrill Company in Wilton, Connecticut, makers of Lavoris mouthwash, received a call from the Tampa police department: A man who had bought a bottle of Lavoris in a nearby supermarket and gargled with it was now seriously ill.

Richardson-Merrill had been beset with other recent product tamperings, and so they put their emergency plan into immediate action. One of their top product research scientists caught the first plane down to Tampa; so did the account executive of the company's public relations counseling firm.

What they learned in Tampa was that the previous Saturday night a traveling salesman had purchased a bottle of Lavoris, which is a bright red liquid. The original contents had somehow been replaced with red muriatic acid, a powerful fluid commonly used as a paint remover. Back in his room, the salesman gargled with the substance and badly burned his esophagus.

Thorough checking and testing of all the other bottles of Lavoris on that supermarket's shelves, and in other supermarkets and drugstores in the area, convinced the police that the tampered bottle was an isolated incident. The public relations consultant persuaded the police that more harm than good would result if the story were given to the press. And the traveling salesman, after being treated with an antidote, was released from the hospital and left town. (He apparently had been out carousing that Saturday night before he bought the tampered mouthwash and so did not want any attention drawn to himself.)

No other tampered Lavoris bottles were discovered, and the incident faded away. This example of publicity avoidance required fast action and good judgment on the part of the manufacturer, the retailer, and the public authorities. In the highly charged atmosphere of public fear over widespread product poisoning that existed in those days, this isolated incident, if mishandled, could have caused long-term damage to the brand name and the company's reputation, as well as creating panic in the city and even the country as a whole.

For the most part, law enforcement and public health officials seem to agree that caution should be used in notifying the public of a product-tampering incident. In fact, the FDA receives several dozen tampering alerts per year—far more than the public ever learns about. One reason officials tread so carefully is that public revelation of such incidents often leads to others—so-called copycat crimes.

Ten years ago, product tamperings were largely unknown. Product recalls, of course, were more common. With the botulism scares of the seventies, particularly affecting canned mushrooms, the public suffered a loss of innocence and was forced to realize that just because a product was sealed in an airtight container did not mean it was safe to eat.

With the growing frequency of deliberate contamination of products, "tamperproof" packaging was developed. The difficulty many people experience in opening these sealed, stamped, glued, stapled, and shrink-wrapped packages may provide a false sense of security. Packaging can only be made tamper-resistant—each package would have to be sold with an armed guard included to be truly tamperproof. Manufacturers themselves are well aware that tamper-resistant measures can be overcome, but obviously, they are not about to reveal exactly how it is done. For our purposes, it's safe to say that no package or container is impregnable. Devising ways to overcome safeguards requires a high degree of ingenuity, but even so, there is always the likelihood that some clever nut will figure it out, and the nightmare will begin.

As in all crises, a major objective should be communicating three crucial attributes to authorities and particularly the public: concern, cooperation, and candor. Note, however, that candor does not always mean being an open book. It was in no one's interest to be completely candid in the Richardson-Merrill incident. By *candor*, we mean always telling the truth. Lies have a way of coming back to haunt you.

Certainly, the most efficient means of communicating these attributes is through the media, but that means letting them "translate" the story. You may wish to communicate directly to key audiences—mailgrams to important customers or retailers are usually effective, and they allow you to get your points across unfiltered.

Remember: Unlike environmental contamination, which is usually seen as a callous (if not willful) disregard for the public, a case of product tampering places you in the role of victim in the public's eyes. Most people will accept the idea that control of a product by the manufacturer ends once it leaves the plant, with one notable exception: Customers will be quick to notice whether you have taken adequate tamper-resistant measures in packaging your products. (If you purvey edible products or over-the-counter pharmaceuticals and are not taking some precautions against tampering, you are acting recklessly from the standpoint of both the public welfare and your company's reputation.)

The decision by Johnson & Johnson (J&J) to pull Tylenol capsules from the over-the-counter market after several tampering incidents was painful, but effective. Public confidence in J&J and the believability of its stated concern for the public was heightened—apparently enhancing sales of other J&J products. That was an extreme solution, but after two spates of tampering, the company felt it had little choice: To continue selling the non-prescription capsules could expose the public to risk and the company to grave liability.

Whatever actions your company is forced to take, and regardless of how an incident is ultimately resolved, product tampering will affect your company's health, too. Your employees will be particularly affected. People like to believe that "their" company is contributing something beneficial to society, and they like outsiders to share that view. Generally, within 48 hours of the revelation of a tampering incident, the public has made up its mind about how it feels about your company, and these impressions will color everything you do thereafter. It is crucial that your company be positioned properly because your response to a tampering incident (or any other crisis, for that matter) will affect both the internal and external perception of the company, and employee morale may suffer as a result.

Also, almost invariably, a suggestion that a product may have been deliberately contaminated by an employee will find its way into the media. Naturally, such a suggestion breeds resentment, suspicion, and fear.

So, employees should be kept as up-to-date on developments during a crisis as possible. You may not be able to reveal any more to employees than you would to the press, but it sounds better coming from management than from the morning paper. Employees should know that their jobs are not in jeopardy, that the tampering was accomplished by an outsider (if that is absolutely confirmed), and that the company is doing what it can to assist the victims and their families. These are the same messages you'll be conveying to the outside world, too.

Coping: The Crisis Plan

Determining how a product can be violated is but one step of a process that is growing more common in the corporate world today: the development of elaborate "crisis plans" in an attempt to be prepared for the worst.

Of course, it's impossible to be fully prepared for all varieties of crises that may occur, but, particularly in the case of a tampering incident, there are some common denominators that can be anticipated. Some public relations agencies now offer as a service the development of these plans. Typically, the service involves hypothesizing what could go wrong, and then developing a plan to deal with it.

The most comprehensive plans include specifications for a "crisis command center," with checklists for staffing (management, secretaries, couriers) and equipment (word processors, facsimile transmitters, tape recorder-equipped telephones). But even without such a center, certain crucial resources can be assembled now to save time and energy later.

For example, have you prepared a list of people who would be considered essential personnel in the event of a crisis? Does this list include home addresses and telephone numbers, and have these people installed answering machines on their home telephones? Crises can develop at all hours of the day and night—vital personnel might have to be reached in the small hours or on weekends. Similarly, are the telephone numbers of officials of the Food and Drug Administration, state health department, Center for Disease Control, and other relevant agencies at hand? Is there a procedure for reaching officials after hours?

You'll also want to have the names and telephone numbers of several laboratories around the country who can perform analyses on short notice. And because a major product tampering incident will require communicating with the outside world, the telephone numbers (both voice and facsimile) of major media should be on file. Contrary to your feelings in the midst of a crisis, the media may be among your best friends.

Although many companies have reviewed their potential vulnerabilities and formulated crisis plans, these plans tend to end up buried in credenzas. The truth is that until you have actually lived through a crisis, it's hard to understand how much of a head start such a plan can provide.

One way to get a sense of it is to stage a drill. Again, some public relations agencies now stage such drills, which include developing a "worst case scenario" and simulating developments in response to management's actions. Such drills can help demonstrate the near-hysteria that can occur when everything seems to go wrong all at once—and the need for creating a response mechanism in advance.

The stakes are high. Market share lost as a result of a tampering incident can take years to recover. Product lines can be eliminated (as with Tylenol capsules), and companies can go out of business in a matter of weeks if a crisis is handled badly. On the other hand, while a crisis would hardly be characterized as an edifying experience, proper and effective response to one can demonstrate (as it did for Johnson & Johnson) the proficiency and leadership of your management. The same holds true for the manner in which you deal with an environmental crisis.

Environmental crises and product tampering, then, share certain features—the health risk foremost among them. Both also focus intense public attention on your company—particularly management. Will it look competent or inept?

You can help tip the balance if you have been carefully managing your corporate impact all along. For example, in a crisis you will rely on the media to help you reach as many people as possible with news of your cooperation, concern, and specific remedial action. Knowing that, it doesn't make much sense to antagonize or simply ignore the media the rest of the time. If the press has seen your company as arrogant in the past, you will probably not be portrayed sympathetically when you need help.

Similarly, if you are not an active participant in the affairs of your local community, how can you expect it to rally behind you in a crisis? Even if you are a major employer, a crisis can sometimes be seen as the result of a reckless action on your part, one that has jeopardized the future of the company and therefore the jobs of hundreds of residents. Politicians have enough targets to shoot at without adding your company to their hit lists—why offer yourself as a sacrifice? Instead, why not help politicians look smart for standing behind you in a crisis? They won't do so unless you have actively supported them previously.

ACQUIRED IMMUNE DEFICIENCY SYNDROME (AIDS)

As we mull over the communications challenges facing managers today, perhaps none is as difficult to grapple with as Acquired Immune Deficiency Syndrome (AIDS).

Think it can't happen to your company? Think again. By the time this book was being written (mid-1988), over 60,000 cases of AIDS had been diagnosed in the United States to date. More than half those victims are already dead. By 1991, it is projected, 250,000 cases will have been identified, and some 50,000 are expected to die that year alone.

The two main communications challenges presented by AIDS are fear and, inevitably, grief—a potent combination.

When an employee (through a voluntary or accidental revelation) is known to be afflicted with AIDS, reactions range from sympathy to hysteria. Workers may demand that AIDS sufferers be barred from the work place, in spite of the growing preponderance of evidence that the disease is not transmitted through casual contact. How management handles the situation can have far-reaching consequences.

Fewer than 10 percent of American companies have succeeded in defining a comprehensive policy toward AIDS.

Perhaps this is because, at this point, the disease is still so new to the workplace that no policy statement can respond to the many different problems that arise when an employee develops symptoms. Visible AIDS symptoms—lesions, weight loss, and such—are generally present in the most advanced stages of the disease. At this point, the employee may not be physically capable of performing his or her job, and many companies have elected to classify these advanced stages of AIDS as they would any other debilitating illness—as a long-term disability. The employee receives disability compensation and is removed from the workplace. As a rule, the policy is acceptable to afflicted employees.

The most difficult AIDS-related challenge facing managers is only beginning to become apparent. As new therapies are being developed to combat AIDS, employees who have been exposed to the AIDS virus but who may not be exhibiting any signs of the disease are undergoing treatment. The drug azidothymidine (AZT), currently in testing stages, is being taken by people who have exhibited no symptoms at all—in fact, it is hoped that people who take AZT *before* symptoms appear will never exhibit symptoms.

As is often the case with drugs undergoing clinical testing, AZT must be taken in precise dosages at precise intervals. Patients often wear alarms to remind themselves to take their medication. Coworkers will quickly come to understand what such alarms signify. Also, AZT, which was originally developed to treat another ailment (unsuccessfully, it turned out), is at this time only used for the treatment of AIDS. In companies where health-insurance reimbursements are handled by company personnel (as opposed to a third-party plan administrator), reimbursement for AZT prescriptions will quickly tip off those company personnel that an employee is being treated for some AIDS-related ailment.

The net result is that at some point, a perfectly healthy-looking employee, who is performing well in his or her job, will be identified as an AIDS patient, and a number of issues will have to be confronted.

Putting the AIDS issue aside for a moment, recall that the most likely candidates to contract AIDS are those who have had homosexual contacts or who are intravenous drug users or those who have had sexual relations with either of these groups.

When it becomes known that an employee has developed AIDS, there is a double shock for coworkers: (1) that the employee has the disease and (2) that he or she has participated in the types of activities that would result in exposure to AIDS in the first place. This latter point may not seem like such a big deal to residents of major metropolitan areas, but in smaller communities around the country, these behaviors are not always well accepted. If youngsters being treated for hemophilia, who have contracted the disease through blood transfusions, have become pariahs in their hometowns, can we expect better attitudes toward AIDS patients who have contracted the disease through homosexual activity?

Coworkers (some at least) will react in a highly emotional manner. They may demand that the employee be fired, or at least assigned to another area of the company where he or she "can't give it to anybody." Failure to deal with these

most vociferous employees can have dramatic consequences. In 1987, a family was literally burned out of their
south Florida home when the parents attempted to send
their sons, both hemophiliacs and both AIDS sufferers, to
the local school. That same uninformed, fear-provoked
response to AIDS could be a disaster for your business, too.

As has been repeatedly said by authorities on the disease,
the most immediate need is to educate the entire population about AIDS: what it is and how it is (and is not)
contracted. This educational process will be more effective if it is undertaken *before* an employee is known to
have the ailment. Public health authorities can assist you
in briefing employees and in preparing materials. Be sure
you deal with the question of what your company feels its
obligations are to the afflicted employee and to his or her
coworkers.

If the employee is involved in any way with the preparation of, for example, food products or medications, you
might be tempted to transfer him or her from that job to
another. Don't even try—it is against the law. Your challenge is to make coworkers and customers comfortable
with the fact that the AIDS-afflicted employee cannot
transmit the disease through the normal course of his or
her job.

Think about the message you will be sending to other
employees by the manner in which you deal with an
employee with AIDS. Most will be appreciative of efforts
on your part to be supportive and accommodating, so long
as they feel secure that they are not themselves at risk. In
the final analysis, that may well be the hardest part of
dealing with AIDS.

Remember, too, that at this writing, AIDS is progressive and nearly always fatal. Chances are, your AIDS-afflicted employee will die from the disease. He or she needs the same kind of compassionate treatment you would afford to the sufferer of any other terminal illness. But don't be lulled into thinking that this disease can be handled in the same manner as, say, terminal cancer.

One of the most tragic developments we have witnessed is that of the AIDS sufferer, already depressed by the knowledge that he or she has a probably fatal illness and possibly rejected by his or her own family, who becomes the focus of coworkers' fear and hatred. The AIDS victim in those circumstances is at the vortex of an ugly, public controversy in the place where most of us spend the bulk of our conscious time—the place of business.

In some towns or cities, and depending on what your company produces, word of an employee with AIDS symptoms will be news, and you may expect press inquiries. A "stand-by statement" should be made ready, not to be distributed to the media, but to have at hand should press calls come in. The statement should describe the company's policy on the issue and note that because the disease is not transmitted through normal conduct of business, no one need be concerned about whether an employee has the ailment or not. It is not the company's business to confirm or deny that a specific employee does or does not have symptoms of AIDS.

Finally, remember that employees who die of AIDS (or any other illness) leave behind friends and coworkers who will mourn the loss of their associate. In a large company, over time, several AIDS deaths could occur. Be especially sensitive of employees' feelings. Circulate a memo, for instance, noting the time and place of the funeral. If donations have been requested in lieu of flowers, a contribution from the company in the name of all employees will be appreciated by both the employees and the survivors.

Keep abreast of new developments in AIDS research and help your employees stay informed. Remember that compassion and decency are usually the first AIDS casualties.

CAUGHT IN THE ACT

Crime pays.

Now we know that statement flies in the face of everything we've all heard since elementary school, but face it, crime pays—in a big way.

Many citizens depend on crime for a livelihood. In the public sector, they include judges, clerks, bailiffs, prosecutors, defenders, police officers, meter maids, and many other federal, state, and local employees. Then there's the private sector: more lawyers, bail bondsmen, locksmiths, and insurance agents.

But consider who benefits more than almost anybody else from the existence of crime, criminals notwithstanding: the media.

Crime sells papers. Lurid stories of gruesome villainy make for attention-getting headlines. "Headless Body in

Topless Bar!" cried the New York *Post* a few years ago. Rupert Murdoch's worldwide empire was built on the like.

Yet in New York and most big cities where violent crime is an unfortunately common occurrence, a standard street murder is no longer a hot news item. That doesn't mean, though, that the media ignore violence.

The real juicy copy comes not from the depravity of the drug-crazed murderer—he's just a spot news item—but from the Fortune 500 company top executive who is caught bribing an official of a West African nation to secure a contract to supply suppositories. Now that's hot news.

From the moment he's arrested, every move this danger-to-society makes will be chronicled: his arraignment and release on his own recognizance; his temporary leave of office until he is "fully vindicated"; his court appearance and plea of *nolo contendere*; and subsequent resignation "for the good of the company."

We're not dismissing the seriousness of the crime of bribery of public officials, American or otherwise, but as an offense against society, it seems to draw a disproportionate share of opprobrium from all quarters.

Why this is so may have to do with the violation of a bond of trust, a bond of perhaps questionable foundation. It assumes that people in high places play by a loftier set of rules. As we have seen, sometimes they don't. Because we measure our governmental and business leaders against a higher standard than we measure ourselves, it's big news when such a leader is shown to have slipped, to have strayed from the straight and narrow. "Who done it" is often more newsworthy than "what was done."

Rather than trying to undertake a sociological analysis of this phenomenon, we can simply accept it—it is the way things are. Which means that the revelation of criminal acts in your corporate corridors, traumatic though they may be as legal crises, become public relations nightmares, especially because in matters of public opinion you can't escape on a technicality. If the public feels you did it, you did it.

That doesn't mean that you can't engender public sympathy for the extenuating circumstances that forced you to violate that trust. Appearing to be genuinely contrite over an error in judgment is often effective, though this tack requires the consumption of a fairly generous serving of humble pie.

As with any crisis, the best way to survive the revelation of criminal behavior within your company is to display candor—though not to the point of creating more concern than an incident warrants. The objective is to get the incident off the front page as quickly as possible so that you can begin the work of restoring the corporate image to its rightful state.

As soon as you learn that there may be a problem, even if the press has yet to catch on to it, you should quietly investigate how extensive the problem is and determine how best to remedy any damage. In spite of your best efforts, though, the news may leak out, often in a distorted fashion. If there is an arrest made, the incident instantly becomes public. In other cases, a disgruntled or perhaps idealistic employee may tip off the press. However the news first spreads, you need to be prepared for the inevitable onslaught of reporters looking for the inside story.

If you have advance knowledge of the incident, you have some advantage. You can take the time you need to form a candid statement that nonetheless supports the good image of the company.

If the reporters' line of questions comes as a shock to you, don't shoot from the hip in return. Tell them you will get back to them as soon as you have had time to review the situation—then start digging.

When you are sure that you have uncovered the facts of the incident in your company, meet with the press and speak frankly about what happened and how you intend to ensure that nothing like it ever happens again.

How candid should you be? To use a slightly grisly analogy, if given a choice, would you prefer to have your leg amputated above the knee in one two-hour surgical procedure or have it hacked off an inch at a time over the course of several weeks by someone who isn't quite sure where to aim the blade? That's what it feels like to have a story pried out by reporters, who view each successive nugget of information as a major prize to be displayed across the front page or the six o'clock news.

If you give the media everything all at once, chances are the story will blow over more quickly. The alternative—to let the press pry details from you and other sources over several days or even weeks—pretty much ensures the continuity of the story, perhaps even front-page news for an extended period.

Two opposing examples of dealing with unpleasant criminal charges were provided recently by the Bank of Boston and Beechnut Nutrition Corporation.

Bank of Boston was accused of participating in a conspiracy to conceal the ownership of what turned out to be money generated through organized crime. When the story broke, Bank of Boston immediately called upon its outside public relations counsel to suggest a strategy. The agency recommended full disclosure to the reporters as soon as possible. When sufficient facts were in hand, a press conference was held. The president of the bank was coached in how best to respond to sticky questions, and as a result, the story quickly moved to the back pages and then faded away. Even the jokes about how "Bank of Boston makes money the old-fashioned way—they launder it!" did not last long.

We should note, as a footnote to our previous discussions of candor, that Bank of Boston did make one false step: Early on in the process, the Bank announced that only two or three employees had been involved. Just a few days later, it was forced to admit that the number was closer to a dozen or so. For the most part, though, they handled a potentially disastrous situation quite well.

Contrast that relatively happy ending with the hapless performance of Beechnut. Accused of selling a cheaper, chemical-based ersatz juice with hardly any apple in it as 100 percent pure apple juice for babies, the company denied any wrongdoing well past the point when its executives were being indicted for fraud.

Months went by during which the company continued to deny the charges. Finally, after the senior executives of the company were found guilty of hundreds of counts of fraud, Beechnut admitted that there might have been a problem, but insisted that measures had been taken. They asked consumers to trust Beechnut once again. Sorry guys, you should have shut the barn door before the horse ran off with your product!

As a whole, Americans are a remarkably forgiving lot. It has been suggested that Richard Nixon could have skirted past the entire Watergate mess had he simply admitted to an error of judgment on the part of his staff and promised that it would never happen again. By stonewalling and obfuscating, Mr. Nixon allowed the incident to be blown bizarrely out of proportion—to the point where even staunch Republicans gave up on him.

Instead of filing charges against your company in general, the authorities may reach into the organization and indict a particular executive for wrongdoing in the course of performing his or her job. Your first reaction may be to jump to the defense of your colleague. Be careful of what you say.

It is okay to say that everyone is shocked that Mr. Smith has been indicted; that you are anxious to clear up the matter as soon as possible, as is Mr. Smith; and furthermore, that Mr. Smith has assured you that he will be vindicated.

After that, it is inappropriate for you to comment on a case under investigation or in litigation. If one person has been indicted, other indictments may follow, and any official comments by the company may haunt you—and possibly hurt you—later on. Always privately assume the worst and disprove it before going public. It if turns out that Mr. Smith has to do a little time in the Big House, your admirable statements supporting him to the last will at best look naive and perhaps even purposely misleading.

Occasionally, an employee is arrested for alleged criminal activity outside work. In such a case, it is not appropriate for the company to comment.

Whether the incident concerns the company as a whole or just one or two employees, remember that the employee grapevine can churn out some of the most amazing permutations of the truth in a very short time (i.e., if $3000 is missing from petty cash, don't be surprised if the story comes back around as involving $300,000 missing from the corporate account, and the president with it.) It is a good idea to make known the basic facts of the case just to hold speculation in check. In addition, employees should be asked to refer any inquiries they may receive from the media or other outsiders to a central location—the head of public relations or the president's office.

Direct communications with stakeholders, including major customers and investors, may be in order if the incident has significant potential implications for the conduct of business. Again, you cannot afford to prejudice the case, but you can reassure these audiences that you are cooperating with authorities and will endeavor to resolve the situation with a minimum of impact on operations. If necessary, assure customers that you are reviewing all accounts to ensure that everything is in order.

11

Self-Destructive Public Relations

How Awry Can Go the Best Laid Plans

For the most part, we've examined how a well-planned and integrated approach to communications in general, and public relations specifically, can help to enhance the corporate identity in good times and protect and preserve it in tough times. Public relations tactics are tools, and like any tools, they can be used correctly or incorrectly.

In the latter case, the damage is usually not too serious, but occasionally the whole ball of yarn can unwind.

OFF ON THE WRONG FOOT

Sam Jones, president of Dedmete Industries, smiled as he walked down the corridor toward his office. The reason he smiled wasn't because it was such a nice day (although it was a beautiful spring morning). Nor was he smiling because the company's quarterly results were looking very healthy (although they were, in fact, well up from last year). Even the fact that, with his new putter, he had broken 80 for the first time ever the previous afternoon was not the main reason for the wide grin he sported.

Sam Jones was smiling because his feet felt great. That was the best news he could have asked for since he was wearing a prototype pair of Dedmete running shoes. These were the most comfortable running shoes he had ever worn. Better still, tests proved that consumers liked them, too, and a new manufacturing process made them so durable that each pair of "Dedmete Dynamos" (as they were to be called) would carry an unconditional, one-year, money-back guarantee, an industry first. Yep, he had a lot to smile about.

As Jones reached his office, he received a telephone call from his public relations consultant, who also had a prototype pair and was equally enthusiastic. The account executive had learned that *Consumer Interest Magazine* was planning a feature article in which it would rate various running shoes currently on the market. Although the testing had been going on for over two months, the account executive had persuaded the editor that the report would be incomplete if it did not contain a review of the new Dedmete Dynamos. The editor agreed to test the shoes personally if the company could provide him with a pair the next day.

Jones was wary. The shoes weren't even in production yet; his production people were still working out the final bugs in the manufacturing process. Still, the magazine had a three-month lead time, and what a way to kick off the introduction of the Dedmete Dynamos! What the heck. He boxed up a pair in the editor's size and sent them out by air express.

Three months passed, and Jones awaited the imminent publication of *Consumer Interest* with acute excitement. The editor (per the magazine's policy) had refused to discuss where Dedmete Dynamos ranked in the test results, but over a recent two-martini lunch with the account executive, he had winked and said he didn't think Dedmete would be disappointed.

At last the issue hit the stands. Lo and behold, Dedmete Dynamos were the top-rated shoe in the survey, far and away. The editor gushed about their style and comfort and the way they were built to last. "It is as if," the editor concluded, "the shoes were handmade. And, though the company hasn't officially announced it, they're planning to offer an unconditional, one-year, money-back guarantee with each and every pair. Run, don't walk," he implored, "to your athletic footwear retailer and get a pair of Dedmete Dynamos, the best running shoe ever made in the U.S.A.!"

What with the fitness craze and all, the story was noted by virtually all the major business media, who promptly pulled together features about Dedmete, the new *wunderkind* in the lucrative running-shoe market. Dedmete stock soared.

Jones took the entire production and marketing staffs to lunch. Everyone was jubilant. Everyone, that is, except Rifkin, a bespectacled, nerdy type from R&D.

"What's wrong?" asked Jones. "You read what they said, the shoes fit 'as if they were handmade.'"

"They *were* handmade, remember?" said Rifkin. "We still don't know if we can make them as good by machine."

"Aw, Rifkin," said Jones, elbowing him as they stumbled out of the restaurant into the blazing light of day. "I know you won't let us down."

Within a couple of weeks, dealers had ordered thousands of pairs of Dedmete Dynamos. Dedmete still didn't have a plant tooled to crank them out. Jones called an emergency meeting with the production team.

With orders flooding in and no way to fill them, Dedmete

had to find an alternate manufacturing technique and a plant that could start filling orders in a hurry. "Every time someone goes into a store and can't get Dynamos, he buys Nikes or New Balance instead," Jones yelled.

Production found two plants, one in Madagascar and another in Brazil, that could begin turning the wheels within 15 days if the design of the shoe were modified—just a teeny weeny bit; no one would ever see the difference. Engineering "SWAT" teams were dispatched east and south. Miraculously, just six weeks later, shoes were enroute to stores. Dealers reported that the new Dynamos were selling out before they were even unpacked—people just plunked down $75 and left their names.

Meanwhile, with the pressure off, Dedmete was able to get their own plant up and running and planned to be shipping the original Dedmete Dynamos within 60 days at the outside. The crisis solved, Jones had time to see how far below 80 he could take his rejuvenated golf game.

This example shows how quick thinking and fast action can get a company through a sticky . . . .

But wait! There's a little more.

About two months later, Jones learned that the first pair of Dynamos had been returned by a dealer, with a friendly note. "A customer brought these back today. As you can see, they've hardly been worn, but the stitching has unraveled completely. I'm sure this pair was that proverbial one-in-a-million, so please issue me a credit. I have given the customer a new pair."

Within a few weeks, incoming shoes outnumbered outgoing three to one. Most of the returns looked like souvenirs from Washington's winter at Valley Forge.

The trade press caught on to the story first. Then *Runner's Planet Magazine* put a little note in its gossip column. A major blow was the *Wall Street Review* article quoting a retailer as saying, "Dedmete Dynamos? You mean Dedmete DOAs. We stopped carrying them. Couldn't make any money on them, what with the postage back and forth to the company and all."

But the worst cut was the editorial in *Consumer Interest*, which lambasted Dedmete for trying (apparently successfully) to dupe the magazine, and thus the public, by passing off prototypes as production models.

Once again, all the major business publications took note. A star has fallen, they intoned.

The Dedmete plant was now up and running, but no one would buy the shoes. Running-shoe sales plummeted. Even worse, bowling shoes and ballet points were off 50 percent, too, although nothing had changed with them. Retailers just weren't buying from Dedmete. The layoffs began.

Not surprisingly, Dedmete stock proved to be a bust on Wall Street. *Corp. Magazine* ran a feature called: "What Happened to Dedmete—and Whose Fault Was It?" Cruelest of all for Jones was the news that a major New England business school was thinking about using Dedmete as a case study in its M.B.A. program—the ultimate indignity.

A year later, as Dedmete was still refunding money under the industry's first (and last) unconditional one-year guarantee, the venerated Amalgamated Sole Corp. consummated a friendly acquisition of Dedmete. Jones, though still smarting, realized enough on the deal to retire, but he hangs around as a consultant three days a week to the Dedmete Division of AmSole.

This ridiculous story is essentially true—such a fiasco actually happened to a leading athletic shoe manufacturer. May it also serve as a reminder that the media exist, it seems, both to revel in the airy heights of your triumph and to rub your nose in the mire of your failure. Don't expect to get great coverage in "up" times and then be ignored when the tide turns. Business failures often make for even better reading than successes, and they may have even more lasting impact.

Not surprisingly, Dedmete's problems began with the best of intentions. The *Consumer Interest* profile was a terrific opportunity—but one that came along too soon. Be philosophical; other opportunities always come along. Instead, Dedmete pulled the trigger too soon, and lost. In our sad scenario, Jones really shot himself in the foot, so to speak, since he managed to alienate every major audience he had: retailers and their customers; the media; the investment community; and, of course, his laid-off employees.

Dedmete might have turned itself around with time, but it's not likely the company or its shoes will be seen again soon in *Consumer Interest*. Too bad, considering the publication's apparent clout with consumers.

The Dedmete example took place over several months. Real public relations faux pas often unfold much more quickly.

Chapter 11

OUT OF STEP WITH
THE TIMES

The following is quite a different example of a self-inflicted mortal wound to one's image. This time it was not actually perpetrated by a corporation per se, but by a well-known institution nonetheless: New York's famed Radio City Music Hall Rockettes.

Remember the Rockettes? That lissome line of long-limbed ladies has opened Radio City's annual Christmas show for some 50 years. Some think the Rockettes are the quintessential New York attraction; others see them as an unspeakably sexist anachronism. Whatever they are, they are union members first.

For some time, the Rockettes had been signing a three-year contract with Radio City that provided for a guaranteed minimum number of performances and other stipulations pertaining to lucrative product endorsements. In fact, even the least-senior dancers earned considerably more than the typical union member—dancer or teamster—which made it hard for the music hall to remain competitive with other New York City venues.

When contract talks reached an impasse, the Rockettes threatened to picket Radio City. The tactic seemed to make sense: In the late seventies, when Rockefeller Center was about to close the music hall forever, it was the Rockettes who danced on the sidewalks of Sixth Avenue, calling attention to the situation and creating such a public outcry that the hall was saved.

Surely Radio City would buckle under the glare of publicity. The Rockettes counted on their unique place in the sentimental hearts of New Yorkers to pressure Radio City to settle quickly.

As lunchtime crowds from the immense skyscrapers poured outside and milled around the plazas of Sixth Avenue, the fur-draped, bejeweled, and high-heeled Rockettes paraded with picket signs under the marquee. The media, especially TV, were out in force to record the event. But, instead of quizzing the Rockettes about their plight, the cameras taped the other women on Sixth Avenue. Many of these women—tweed-suited, buttoned-down corporate types—saw themselves as embroiled in a continuing struggle to advance through the ranks of the male-dominated corporate world.

Women who believed they must fight every day to be taken seriously at work were not amused by the sight of a "bunch of airheads trying to attract a crowd," as one passerby suggested. They said it was trivial. They said it was demeaning to all women. It has been suggested that the Rockettes were a little out of touch with their constituency.

Capitalizing on their outrageous good luck, Radio City management provided a spokesman who rationally and quietly explained that the Rockettes were not being eliminated, nor even threatened. Radio City desired only to treat all union performers (a little redundancy there) on a parity basis.

The Rockettes are nothing if not quick learners. They were out there again the next day but this time dressed in old clothes and worn shoes. Too late. The news media were already onto another story—the Rockettes picketing was now old news. In a stunning turnaround, public sympathy sided with management, and the contract that was eventually signed by Radio City and the Rockettes was much closer to what management had sought than anyone had thought possible.

IN THE SOUP

Once upon a time the packaged soup business was almost totally dominated in the United States by Campbell Soup. The company made canned condensed soups, and some of their varieties commanded as much as a 95 percent share of the market.

But Campbell's soup products could make very little headway in Europe, where the market was dominated by Knorr, a German Swiss manufacturer of dehydrated or powdered soups. Knorr did not make canned soups, and Campbell did not make dehydrated soups.

Then one day a breakthrough idea occurred to Corn Products Company, the big, U.S.-based international food manufacturer that owned Knorr. Corn Products had been observing the gradually increasing sales of Knorr dehydrated soups among the little gourmet food specialty shops in New York City, Washington, and a selected few other cities in the United States. Why not try to sell the wonderfully varied Knorr dehydrated soups in supermarkets all across the country? Knorr has been so successful in keeping Campbell from making headway in Europe, it might be able to beat Campbell head-to-head in the United States as well.

Of course, there were certain problems in mass marketing a packaged dehydrated soup in a country where customers were used to opening a can, adding an equal quantity of water, and heating the mixture for 3 to 4 minutes. Knorr's dehydrated gourmet-style soup took 12 to 15 minutes to prepare. And the desiccated dust that fell from the envelope into the pot wasn't very eye-catching.

Nevertheless, the end result in Europe, and for the wealthy American housewives who patronized the food boutiques, was so much better than the plebeian Campbell concoction that Corn Products management determined to give it a go. A real big go.

They built a building at the site of their huge corn-grinding operation in Argo, Illinois, and they installed there the most modern dehydrating equipment and dry-mixing facilities available. They designed new, brilliantly attractive packages and started filling the pipelines.

Meanwhile, Campbell, taking note of this major threat to their souply hegemony, decided to engage Corn Products in a rearguard action in the United States. They hastily threw together their own line of dehydrated soups and named it "Red Kettle." Their strategy was clearly to divert some of the interest that Corn Products would arouse in the new convenience soup category to their own dried line with the better known Campbell's brand on it.

Corn Products, in turn, decided to trump that action by rushing their new made-in-America Knorr line to the food stores without even test marketing it. They did not want to let the Red Kettle line get started until they were well underway.

A big press conference was staged in New York to announce the new line of soups. Magazine and newspaper food editors were feted with every variety Knorr was introducing. All kinds of nutritional and taste advantages were imputed to this powdered miracle with the great European heritage. Even European cooks were imported to serve the exotic potions and show new ways to use soup in meals.

Then the trade advertising campaign was launched, followed closely by the national advertising wave. Every effort was expended by the Corn Products salespeople to get important supermarket shelf space for the new line of soups.

Stories were developed about the history of Knorr and the care with which the soup ingredients were grown, selected, and blended, cooked, and then dehydrated, packaged, and shipped in Europe. Now these same conditions were being duplicated, and even improved upon, in the United States with the aid of modern technology. The dehydrater in Argo was absolutely state-of-the-art.

Corn Products executives, in their enthusiasm, seized on the first shipment of the made-in-America Knorr soup packages and sent them to friends and business contacts, as counseled by the public relations staff.

The first indications of trouble came when some of the executives' wives made the soups as the centerpiece of a home meal.

"Kinda crunchy, isn't it?"

"Crunchy? I can't even chew it."

"What's it supposed to taste like?"

"Tastes like colored straw to me."

"Maybe you didn't heat it enough."

"Did it for 25 minutes. The package said 20."

"Maybe you overheated it."

"Those little green buckshot are never going to melt."

"What do you suppose they are?"

"Green pea pellets."

"And those orange shards? Carrots?"

"Let's go out to eat."

The next few days featured reports from all over the country from company salesmen, supermarket managers, and just plain friends of the family. The soups were awful: tasteless, indigestible, and ugly.

What could have happened?

As the investigation started, Corn Products withdrew all the made-in-America Knorr packages they could find. The supermarkets were only too glad to comply. Even the little gourmet delicatessens that still had the imported European-made Knorr soups were getting complaints. Those too stopped selling, as a wave of utter disgust for Knorr products seemed to envelope the American housewife.

Back in Illinois, it was discovered that the state-of-the-art mass-cooking-dehydrating-mixing system, where not a human hand would touch the food, had made the simple mistake of not having a human palate taste it either. Somehow the system never achieved sufficient heat to cook the vegetables, so that when the dehydrater went to work, it toughened up the vegetable flakes, achieving a kind of petrified garden effect.

The result would have fit better into the business end of a rifle than into a soup tureen. Hundreds of thousands of American stomachs testified to that. And the subsequent word of mouth about this curious new product was magnified by the many food editors who had to recant on their columns of praise written after the opening press luncheon.

The very success of the introductory campaign turned in on itself. The flawed product had nowhere to hide.

Not only were millions of dollars in advertising and public relations expenditures wasted, but the expensive new production equipment had to be shut down. The Knorr line was withdrawn pending retooling and re-engineering.

Unfortunately, after the production facilities were working smoother and turning out a satisfactory product, Corn Products management discovered there was no longer a market for Knorr dehydrated soups.

Whereas the company had been able to titillate curiosity about this new process product and whet many sated appetites, they now could only stimulate revulsion. Many people even recoiled at taste-testing a sample when they learned the name of the soup. There was a dearth of second chances being allotted.

Yet in Europe, the locally manufactured Knorr soups continued to sell well. New varieties were developed periodically, and the market continued to grow. Canned soups continued to fail on the Continent.

Slowly, over the past few years, European-made Knorr packaged soups have started to appear again in the gourmet food sections of supermarkets in some big cities. A new generation of cosmopolitan gourmet, seeking a different taste and texture for his/her meals, is tentatively trying these curious dehydrated blends.

Once again, a new generation of management of the parent company is considering a limited manufacturing operation in the United States. But Campbell Soup's Red Kettle line, which has long since been deep-sixed, will be allowed to rest in peace. It served its purpose as an ominous shadow years ago that forced Corn Products into the cauldron before it was ready.

Stay tuned: Campbell Soup is back in 1988 with a new dry soup mix.

THE DARK SIDE

In the chapter on corporate visibility, we discussed the ways in which a company can attract favorable attention to itself by supporting worthwhile causes. So seemingly enlightened is that technique that it was bound to be abused.

A foremost example was provided by the Foundation for Fire Safety (FFS), a nonprofit Washington-based organization. With a name like that—"Foundation" has such a dignified ring to it, and "Fire Safety" is right up there with motherhood and apple pie—it seemed an eminently respectable organization to support. In fact, however, the FFS had a rather unorthodox orientation: It contended that the main fire hazard in America was plastics in the home and office.

The FFS was active in lobbying for limitations in the use of plastics in certain applications—especially the polyvinyl chloride (PVC) pipe used for, among other things, fire sprinkling systems.

Polyvinyl chloride pipe is relatively inexpensive and allows building owners to retrofit existing structures with sprinkler systems at considerably less cost than if they were to use the heretofore standard material, steel conduit. You might expect that such a development would be unpopular with steel-pipe makers, and you'd be right.

As was documented in an exhaustive article in *Fortune Magazine*, the Foundation for Fire Safety received the vast majority of its funding from Allied Tube and Conduit, of Chicago. One can assume that a certain portion of the funding came from unsuspecting folks who thought fire safety sounded like a good idea.

The company was certainly within its rights to support the FFS, but using the guise of a foundation as a front for the company's attempts to hamper competition was a disservice to the many worthy foundations whose work is more altruistic in nature.

To complicate matters further, it was correctly assumed that if the FFS only zeroed in on PVC pipe, its subterfuge would be quickly detected. Thus it spent a great deal of time and money denigrating other plastics as well, such as polyurethane foam—a material that represented no threat to Allied at all.

Using FFS "experts" as spokespeople, print and broadcast journalists produced countless stories about the "hidden terror" in most people's homes—those innocent-looking plastics we all take for granted. Foundation "investigators" raced to the scene of fires that had resulted in multiple fatalities, ready to say on camera that the cause of the deaths "appeared to be related to the deadly plastics in the home." An oft-quoted FFS spokesman insisted that the presence of foam products in most homes was as dangerous as keeping a bucket of gasoline on the living-room floor. There were many other equally egregious examples.

It's often the case that the power of a tactic or technique is most evident when it is used for less-than-admirable purposes, and the Allied/FFS connection is a good example. The effectiveness of this masterfully executed communications strategy has been acknowledged—grudgingly—by almost everyone who has witnessed it.

This is the side of public relations that gives the profession a bad name. It reflects badly on everyone involved, but particularly on the company behind the promotion.

12

Unspontaneous Combustion

The Orchestration of Public Concern

Chapter 12

An incident that left an indelible impression on us happened in the U.S. Senate cloakroom several years ago. A delegation of worried businessmen was visiting a certain famous and powerful southern senator to explain their fears about a pending labor bill.

"Ah thoroughly agree with you-all," intoned the mellifluous legislator. "You-all make excellent points. But ah need mah constituents to force me to vote properly."

"Senator, Ah . . . er . . . I don't understand," said one of the businessmen. "You know what's right, but you can't vote your conscience?"

"Ah know what's right when mah electorate *tells* me what's right. You-all go back on home now and put some pressure on me with some grass-roots support. Ah want to get letters and telegrams by the bushel. Ah want mah office staff buried in telephone calls. Ah want to be able to tell mah home state newspapers how they're beatin' down mah doors. Then Ah'll go out and round up the votes from mah colleagues on the Laybah Committee because Ah'll be driven by messianic zeal. Ah need to be motivated and impelled. Ah want to do the right thing, but you must show me the way."

Thus was born a public relations program cut to fit the prescribed pattern. Those businessmen went back to East Cupcake, Georgia; Wisteria Mills, Mississippi; and Brakedown, Texas. They raised sums of money to print information fliers and got their small-town men's service clubs and women's garden clubs and American Legion posts to begin writing letters and postcards to their congresspeople and senators, hammering on two or three key points in the impending legislation.

The businessmen gave speeches, which were reported in the local weeklies, and clippings of the articles were sent to the mellifluous senator in Washington. His staff kept a running count of the mail, pro and con.

The senator then made speeches about the speeches, and he cited the tenor of back-home comment. He pounded the floor, he got red in the face, and he grabbed other senators by the lapels and bent their ears by the hour. Soon those senators were doing likewise to others, who were also getting cards and letters by the pound.

When the preliminary vote came up in committee, the bill was soundly defeated. Even the *Washington Post* noted the surprising intensity of the opposition. The labor bill's supporters had been caught off guard. They had failed to mount a countervailing outpouring of popular support.

Thus did democracy out that year.

The labor bill that bowed to a swell of public pressure managed to pass in the next session of Congress because its *proponents* prepared properly back in the hustings to get *vox populi* expressed properly.

Point, counterpoint. Pressure and counterpressure. Spontaneity is too important to leave to chance.

All over the country groups come together to argue their case publicly for or against something they feel strongly about, from "Save the Snail Darter" to "Keep Our Bridges Clean." These groups raise money, print leaflets, stage demonstrations for television, distribute buttons. They march; they write letters; they create slogans. They attract attention.

These like-minded people banding together to promote or attack one issue are known as "coalitions." The telephone books are filled with do-for or do-against coalitions, but nowhere more than in Washington, D.C., home of the nation's collective conscience.

Some coalitions are more effective than others in pressing their points. Sometimes this is because they happen to hit upon a sensitive public chord and they develop good resonance. Sometimes the coalitions have an astute media director, and he or she strategically times their demonstrations for the convenience of local TV—like on weak news days, such as Saturday afternoons in the winter.

Indeed, skillful TV news exposure goes a long way toward clarifying an issue. Good media directors know how to think visually and plan according to TV news program deadlines. It has been said that the Vietnam War would still be going if the evening news had not brought the carnage of that conflict into millions of American homes each night.

The orchestration of pressure can take many forms. Labor unions have known the effectiveness of strikes, picket lines, and boycotts for many years. Company managements have tried to match those tactics with lockouts and blacklists.

Organized labor, master at applying pressure, has discovered another way to squeeze company management—apply pressure to the company's outside directors.

The underlying theory is that outside board members often have an important job in their own companies—perhaps as president or chairman—and can be reached through that pressure point.

For example, consider the Hard Tack Grit and Biscuit Company. One of its outside board members also happens to be president of a big insurance company (call it the Guaranteed Life Insurance Company). Let's assume that this insurance company derives much of its income from management of pension funds. Now suppose that several of the biggest of these funds happen to be *union* pension funds.

Assume that a union has a gripe with the company on whose board our insurance company president sits. The "target" company, Hard Tack, is in the food-processing business, and its dispute is with the bakers' union. But unions hang together. The head of the bakers' union talks to the head of the poultry pluckers' union.

Though Guaranteed Life has nothing to do with the bakers' union, it does manage the $400 million crate makers' union pension fund, the $600 million air control assistants' union pension fund, the $550 million egg candlers' pension and welfare fund, and of course, the poultry pluckers' pension fund.

An emissary from the poultry pluckers' union calls on the

president of Guaranteed Life and carefully explains that he has been in touch with all those union presidents, and they are very sympathetic to the cause of the bakers' union versus the Hard Tack Grit and Biscuit Company. So sympathetic are they that they will find it hard to justify continuing to pay management fees and commissions to a company whose top executive is clearly supportive of the rank-and-file baker's deadly enemy.

This leaves the president of Guaranteed Life two choices. Leave the Hard Tack board or get Hard Tack to talk "sense" with the bakers. Otherwise, Guaranteed Life is going to lose some of its biggest pension accounts. Oh, incidentally, those funds might move over to Rest Assured Mutual Life, Guaranteed's biggest competitor.

Faced with this uniquely unpleasant choice, some men and women of great principle have been known to waver. The outside director has a general obligation to remain objective and to act in the best interests of the company on whose board he or she sits. However, it has been pointed out that only a person of intense conviction, or a damn fool, would put directorial duties ahead of responsibilities to one's own company and stockholders. When it comes to fiduciary responsibility, what should be the ultimate guide?

If the unions can bring enough pressure on enough outside board members and resignations start to happen, the resulting burnout will waft its ashes over the labor dispute. Several labor stalemates have been broken in this way.

What does it all mean?

The senator and the director provide two very different, and yet very similar, examples of the application of pressure and the immense power of public opinion. Managing corporate impact demands that you recognize and respect this power.

Early on, we spoke of Newton's Third Law of Motion: Every action has an equal and opposite reaction. Now let's look at the First Law: A body in motion tends to remain in motion; a body at rest tends to remain at rest.

In a republic, the authority to make decisions is granted to a few by the whole. Our electoral process assumes that these few are equipped to deal with the complexities of our society and make rational, *objective* decisions. But the process is somewhat subverted by the fact that these few—our chosen representatives and the civil servants whose jobs they control—are as susceptible to pressure as anyone else, perhaps more so.

Public opinion is usually at the heart of that pressure, and as Newton's Third Law suggests (albeit, in another context), public opinion is not spontaneous, it is orchestrated.

Without an orchestrated effort to arouse it, public opinion remains a body at rest. It takes a catalyst to force people to develop an opinion and ultimately act on it. That catalyst is usually someone who understands that most people, while sympathetic to the misfortunes of others, don't get involved in an issue until it comes home. The activist needs only to show how the average Joe or Jane will be hurt by that issue—nuclear power, neighborhood shelters for the homeless, industrial pollution, legalized abortions, or whatever—and before long, people will rally to the cause.

Public opinion then becomes a body in motion, and a formidable one at that.

These activists or orchestrators include virtually every constituency: business, labor, environmental and consumer activists, old people, gay people, racial minorities, women (generically), homeless people, and so on. Even the media, which serve as primary communications vehicles for these other constituencies, can be an orchestrator unto themselves. The hackneyed image of the crusading reporter, searching as Diogenes did for an honest man, stopped being hackneyed with Vietnam and Watergate.

When the thrust of public opinion is misread, damage can be significant. In Chapter 11, we recounted the story of the Rockettes who, by erring in their assessment of their supposed allies, lost a battle with Radio City management in the space of an hour. The public, whom they had counted on to put pressure on Radio City, sided instead with management. Fighting for the right to work is serious business, and appearing to trivialize it scuttled their strategy.

Another example of the power of public opinion was provided by the ill-fated attempts a few years ago to pass the Equal Rights Amendment (ERA). This seemingly innocuous statement, if passed, would have made discrimination on the basis of one's gender illegal.

Though the ERA should have been able to stand on its own merits, it failed to be ratified by the requisite number of states—even after women's rights activists were able to obtain an unprecedented extension of the ratification process.

While the ERA had the support of the increasingly powerful women's rights lobby, the opposition ultimately proved
to be better financed, better organized, and better con-
nected. The opposition produced scads of women who did
not support the ERA for a variety of reasons and portrayed
those men who did support it as wimps. Although the
amendment most certainly would have had significant
ramifications, a steady stream of ludicrous suggestions
circulated all around the country: It would, critics said,
create unisex public toilets and mixed locker rooms.
Before long, the amendment became the subject of ridi-
cule—men and women alike began to have their doubts
about the whole thing.

Just who was the opposition? Anti-ERA sentiment seemed
to cross all socioeconomic boundaries, but as is often the
case when semisavory tactics are being used to undercut
public support for a proposal, no single organization stood
out as the prime opponent. Influential individuals, however, did have an impact.

For example, a major flap developed over the role of
women in the armed forces. Even ERA proponents con-
ceded that, if passed, the amendment could lead to deploy-
ment of female combat soldiers. Why not, if they are
capable? they said.

While the Armed Forces *per se* did not have an official ERA
stance, highly placed warriors within the ranks of the
Army, Air Force, and Navy (not to mention the American
Legion) popped their collective corks. Soldiering was, and
always had been, a man's game, they said. Firefighters and
police officers offered similar reasons for opposing the
amendment.

When the dust settled, of course, ERA was mortally wounded, although it's likely that at some point we'll see it again. But even though the public in "public opinion" has a relatively short memory, the media have it all on tape to remind us of all the reasons the bill was defeated the first time.

The need for orchestrating public concern is not limited to national issues. Almost any company from time to time needs to broaden its support base in order to accomplish certain goals. In an era of suspicion toward seemingly anything a corporation does or wants to do, there is a need to show how a given proposal will benefit more than the narrow interests of any single entity.

Remember Spotso, our hypothetical soap company that was trying to get a variance? Assuming the zoning mavens are a body at rest and likely to remain so, their natural inclination would be to leave well enough alone if they perceive the sole beneficiary of a change would be one company. What Spotso should do is create and manage public opinion such that the zoning officials would be perceived as acting against the interest of the town by turning down the request.

If Spotso wants a variance to allow fewer but heavier trucks to come and go from its plant, the company should broaden its support base for the plan. For starters, Spotso should speak to local businesses about how the variance would improve traffic flow on Main Street, making it easier for shoppers to get to the stores.

Then, the local Sierra Club office should be shown how

rerouting Spotso traffic will cut down on exhaust emissions downtown.

The town highway superintendent would appreciate the fact that allowing the use of the new trucks would reduce the overall burden on the town's already decrepit streets.

The local school board would be relieved that Spotso trucks would no longer pass the elementary school during lunchtime.

Then, Spotso need ask but one more thing of these people: that they come to the zoning board meeting and speak in favor of the application.

Yes, once again we've over-simplified, but this process is carried out every day by smart managers who understand that a proposal's inherent logic alone is not enough to make it fly. They know they have to have a broader constituency or else they will appear to be acting strictly from self-interest.

The case of the mellifluous southern senator with which we began this chapter, while humorously depicted, is not all that uncommon. Politicians are acutely sensitive to the wishes of their constituents, and the success or failure of many an initiative can hinge on the degree to which it attracts a broad base of support. One of the most effective services provided by Washington lobbying firms (and notably the Washington office of Burson-Marstellar, we judiciously add) is constituency development.

When a company or association is trying to get a particular

bill introduced and eventually passed, such specialists review the proposed legislation closely to discern what third-party organizations would be disposed to support the bill. For example, a bill that would encourage the development of low-cost housing for the elderly could easily get the support of the formidable American Association of Retired Persons if its passage would ultimately reduce the cost of living for retirees.

A less obvious example: Suppose Congress is debating a piece of tax-reform legislation that would change the deductibility of home office equipment. Naturally, the computer industry would be opposed, as one would expect, and its entreaties might well fall upon deaf ears.

But what if there were evidence to show that as more and more professional women are also raising families, many have opted to work at home, either full-time or part-time. If the bill could be shown to have harmful repercussions for this group, the National Organization of Women might well be disposed to speak out against the legislation. So might writers' guilds and associations of consultants (who often work out of their homes). A steady stream of letters to legislators and some well-timed public statements can demonstrate to the lawmakers that this little item could become a real albatross. (Admittedly, this is a very simplistic description of a very sophisticated—and subtle—process. Doing it well requires a lot of expertise. Amateurs can easily get into trouble.)

Conclusion

The Impact of Impact

It turns out that finishing a book is more difficult than starting one, at least if you're the author. We hope that the same is not true for the reader.

We've wandered about somewhat, covering a lot of topics (maybe too many, then again maybe too few), but have always tried to come back to the main point: that managing your corporate impact takes as much work as managing your production line and it's no less important.

For all of you who wondered why we never showed the communications matrix we touted early on, behold! Gratification awaits:

	Quarterly/Annual Results	New CEO	New Product Introduction	Environmental Crisis	Layoffs	Crime	Product Recall	Corporate Philanthropy
Customers	•	•	•	•	•	•	•	•
Employees	•	•	•	•	•	•	•	•
Suppliers	•	•	•	•	•	•	•	•
Wall Street	•	•	•	•	•	•	•	•
Legislators	•	•	•	•	•	•	•	•
Local Community	•	•	•	•	•	•	•	•

In the big picture, everyone needs to know something about nearly everything else. Some may need more or different information than others, but most of your stakeholders are affected in some way by the business decisions you make, and they need to understand how they are affected.

Remember the mosaic. Each tile helps to complete the picture, but few people ever see the whole. Your challenge is to help them see the most important facets of the company so that they can make informed judgments.

As we noted early on, it's probably not possible to hold the hand of every stakeholder to the degree you might wish. At the same time, however, any business decision you make has communications implications for most, if not all, of your stakeholders. Where those implications are most notable—where the risk of confusing or alienating your most important audiences is greatest—that's where you have to focus first. Usually, these primary, "must-reach" audiences are few in number. Taking the time and trouble to ensure that they are on board is worth whatever it costs.

Business challenges abound today. The era when one could come up with a better idea, build it, and sell it with nary a care about such concerns as employee quality of life, environmental impact, or consumer rights has long passed. In fact, ignoring those concerns for decades until severe problems developed contributed greatly to the tempestuous regulatory environment in which we now live. (It also launched the public careers of activists like the late naturalist Rachel Carson and pioneer consumer advocate Ralph Nader.)

As we approach the nineties, it is essential to recognize that all companies, public or private, must answer to more than just consumers. The challenge of meeting the expectations of an increasingly wary public weigh as heavily on most managers as the "normal" problems—for example, production, distribution, and marketing—that they encounter daily. It's the impact of corporate impact, and it may be your biggest challenge of all.

With these challenges come opportunities. By assuming a leadership role within your industry and within your community, you can thrive.

Be guided by three rules of thumb:

- *Know yourself.* Look at your company the way other people do and keep an eye on how the things you do and the ways in which you do them are themselves a form of communication. Are you saying what you mean?
- *Know your audience.* Who are your primary stakeholders, and what do they want to hear? Are you communicating in a manner that makes it easy for them to understand? Are you communicating?
- *Assume the worst.* Take for granted that no matter how hard you try to make your point, someone will misunderstand or ignore it if it suits them to do so. Expect, and keep listening for, signs that your messages are either not reaching their intended audiences or are falling on deaf ears, and if necessary, change the way in which you communicate.

These are not great pearls of wisdom. They're simple, pragmatic rules that can be applied in almost any situation, whether in the course of business-as-usual or in a crisis. And, as too many companies have learned and relearned, ignoring them is a big mistake.

Index

Index

Index

International Nickel Company of
Canada (INCO) example of
hostile takeover, 145
Interviewing
to develop positioning goal, 39–43
one-on-one, 90–91
Investor relations, in Pennzoil-
Texaco debacle, 136–138
Investors
attracting, 121–123
meeting with potential, 124–125
relations with, 131–138
Issues
accounting firm stand on, 165,
167–168
business-related, 63–64
taking stand on, 57–63
underwriting leader of specific,
73–74
Italian corporate takeovers, 148

Japanese corporate takeovers,
148–149
Junk bonds, 152
JWT Group, example of takeover,
156–157

Kohlberg, Kravis, & Roberts (KKR),
139

Labour unions, as pressure groups,
230–232
Lawyers. *See* Attorneys
Legal Staff, 168–169
Leveraged buyout (LBO), 139–141
Litigation, environmental issue,
182–183
Lobbyists, 24–25, 94
public opinion and, 235–238
women's rights, 235–236
Local Emergency Planning
Committees (LEPCs), 175–177

Management buyout (MBO),
139–141
Marketing services. *See* Professional
services, marketing
Media
communicating with, in "going
public," 122
corporate crime and, 202–203,
205–206
improving relations with, 132–133
reaching desired, 25–26
pressure groups and, 230–231
Media alert, 83–85
Medical profession, self promotion
by, 170
Mergers, forced. *See* Takeovers,
hostile
Message consistency, CEO, 27–32

Mutual companies, 127

Newsletter, 94–95
News release. *See* Press release

"Off-the-record" comments, 91
Op-Ed articles, 61, 86–87, 171

Packaging, 41
tamperproof, 191–192
Pennzoil-Texaco, example of poor
investor relations, 136–138
Philanthropy, corporate, 64–70
corporate interests and, 69–70
corporate profits and, 66–67
dividing up funds for, 68
establishing policy for, 65–66
theme of, 68–69
Pitch letter, 89
Pitney Bowes, example of CEO
stand on issues, 59–62
Political action committees (PACs),
94
Politicians
contacting, in face of takeover,
155–156
public opinion and, 237–238
support of, in crises, 196–197
Positioning
corporate, 34
research and 38–43
Presentation in "going public,"
124–125
Press conference, 80
Press contacts, 22–26
Press kit, 86
Press relations, 21–22
consumerism and, 48
Press release, 76–80
corporate visibility and, 55–56
follow up on, 78–79
writing successful, 76–78
Pressure groups, 233–238
Procter & Gamble, logo problem at,
7–9, 54
Product introduction, 19–20
Product tampering, 188–197
consumer reaction to, 188–189
crisis plan for coping with,
194–197
employees and, 193–194
examples of, 189–191
packaging and, 191–192
Product vs. corporate identity, 7–9
Professional leadership, 164–165,
167
Professional services, marketing,
161–172
accountants, 163–168
attorneys, 168–169
general tactics, 170–172